Getting Started in

FUNDAMENTAL ANALYSIS

The *Getting Started In* Series

Getting Started in Online Day Trading by Kassandra Bentley

Getting Started in Asset Allocation by Bill Bresnan and Eric P. Gelb

Getting Started in Online Investing by David L. Brown and Kassandra Bentley

Getting Started in Investment Clubs by Marsha Bertrand

Getting Started in Internet Auctions by Alan Elliott

Getting Started in Stocks by Alvin D. Hall

Getting Started in Mutual Funds by Alvin D. Hall

Getting Started in Estate Planning by Kerry Hannon

Getting Started in Online Personal Finance by Brad Hill

Getting Started in 401(k) Investing by Paul Katzeff

Getting Started in Internet Investing by Paul Katzeff

Getting Started in Security Analysis by Peter J. Klein

Getting Started in Global Investing by Robert P. Kreitler

Getting Started in Futures by Todd Lofton

Getting Started in Financial Information by Daniel Moreau and Tracey Longo

Getting Started in Emerging Markets by Christopher Poillon

Getting Started in Technical Analysis by Jack D. Schwager

Getting Started in Hedge Funds by Daniel A. Strachman

Getting Started in Options by Michael C. Thomsett

Getting Started in Real Estate Investing by Michael C. Thomsett and Jean Freestone Thomsett

Getting Started in Tax-Savvy Investing by Andrew Westham and Don Korn

Getting Started in Annuities by Gordon M. Williamson

Getting Started in Bonds by Sharon Saltzgiver Wright

Getting Started in Retirement Planning by Ronald M. Yolles and Murray Yolles

Getting Started in Online Brokers by Kristine DeForge

Getting Started in Project Management by Paula Martin and Karen Tate

Getting Started in Six Sigma by Michael C. Thomsett

Getting Started in Rental Income by Michael C. Thomsett

Getting Started in Chart Patterns by Thomas N. Bulkowski

Getting Started in Fundamental Analysis by Michael C. Thomsett

Getting Started in

FUNDAMENTAL ANALYSIS

Michael C. Thomsett

WILEY

John Wiley & Sons, Inc.

Published by John Wiley & Sons, Inc., Hoboken, New Jersey.
Published simultaneously in Canada.

For general information on our other products and services or for technical support, please contact our Customer Care Department within the United States at (800) 762-2974, outside the United States at (317) 572-3993 or fax (317) 572-4002.

Wiley also publishes its books in a variety of electronic formats. Some content that appears in print may not be available in electronic books. For more information about Wiley products, visit our website at www.wiley.com.

Library of Congress Cataloging-in-Publication Data:
Thomsett, Michael C.
 Getting started in fundamental analysis / Michael C. Thomsett.
  p. cm.
 Includes index.
 ISBN-13 978-0-471-75446-6 (pbk.)
 ISBN-10 0-471-75446-3 (pbk.)
 1. Investment analysis. 2. Stocks. I. Title.
 HG4529.T487 2006
 332.63'2042—dc22
                              2005027857

Printed in the United States of America.

10 9 8 7 6 5 4 3 2 1

Contents

Introduction: How Fundamental Are the Fundamentals?   1

Chapter 1

Financial Statements and What They Reveal   5

Chapter 2

Basic Stock Market Theories   33

Chapter 3

The Audited Statement—Flawed but Useful   57

Chapter 4

Finding Financial Information Online: Step-by-Step
Explanations   77

Chapter 5

How Accurate Are the Numbers?   95

Chapter 6

Confirmation: The Trend of the Trends   121

Chapter 7

Balance Sheet Ratios: Making the Analysis   137

Chapter 8

Income Statement Ratios: Tracking the Profits   155

Chapter 9

The Popular P/E Ratio and How to Use It   173

Chapter 10

Using Fundamental—and Technical—Analysis Together   187

Chapter 11

Indicators That Go beyond the Statements   201

Glossary   215

Notes   227

Index   229

Getting Started in

FUNDAMENTAL ANALYSIS

How Fundamental Are the Fundamentals?

There is a vast difference between understanding something well enough to buy it as opposed to understanding it well enough to sell it.
—Zig Ziglar, *Secrets of Closing the Sale*, 1984

B asic, obvious, plain, simple—all of these words describe *fundamental* in some way. But in practice it is difficult to decide which stocks to buy, how long to hold onto them, and when or if to sell. The very concept of *value* is itself complex. So when it comes to the market, the "fundamentals" are not always basic, obvious, plain, or simple.

Indeed, they are far from it.

Nevertheless, there is a small but important number of guidelines that you can follow to manage your investment decisions and to reduce and control risk. The fundamentals come in many forms, some complex and some simple. The best-known historical information is still found on a company's financial statements. The summary of what a company owns and owes and its net worth, and the year's operating results are, of course, very revealing because they provide you with the basic (fundamental) view of how all corporate results are measured: by the numbers.

The numbers are never the whole story, only a starting point. Recognizing the complexity of accounting decisions made by a company and its auditors, the timing of when transactions are put into the books, and the internal valuation of assets a corporation uses, all affect the value of a corporation and of its stock. When you look at one company next to another, however, you do not know whether their financial statements were prepared using the same or similar accounting assumptions.

This presents every investor with a serious problem. If one corporation is conservative in the way it prepares its financial reports, but another is aggressive, then you cannot make a meaningful comparison. In this respect, the fundamentals are far from fundamental. The basis for comparison may not even exist, which is why you need to employ specific tools designed to test the numbers. Ratios and trend analyses are among the tools that fundamental analysts use every day. You do not need an accounting education to make informed judgments about the numbers and the trends they represent.

The fundamentals contain far more than just the numbers. For example, most stock market experts would agree that nonfinancial aspects fall within the range of fundamental information. Matters such as management, industry competitive stance, reputation, dividend rate and payment history, and regulatory record, all affect what investors think about companies, even though these data are not strictly financial in nature.

In addition to the fundamentals in a range of information types, investors look at technical information, trends related specifically to market price. It is a mistake to use only one form of analysis to the exclusion of other forms. Both fundamental and technical information are related to one another. In this book you will see why using a combination of fundamental and technical indicators is sensible and provides you with valuable information.

Most investors recognize the importance and value of fundamental analysis but are not sure that they can master its use. Anyone who does not have an accounting education has a sense that fundamental analysis may be too complex. This is not true. Accounting and the reports that are derived from fiscal analysis are complex documents, but you will see in using this book that you do not require an accounting background to benefit from this range of analytical tools.

The sense that it is simply too complex comes from the unfortunate fact that many information sources—such as the Internet, books, magazine articles—either present information in an overly complex format or oversimplify and present the same ratios without giving you any realistic, practical applications. This is unfortunate. Fundamental analysis does not have to be so difficult that you cannot grasp the information and put it to work to manage risks and make informed decisions. Here the information is kept simple and presented with illustrations, examples, checklists, key points, and definitions in context. This helps you move through the chapters, even when simply looking up a concept or to read a section, and then understand how the information is useful to you.

A problem every investor faces in deciding how to analyze stocks is not enough choices. The problem is that there are *too many* choices. There are many viable stocks to choose from, well-managed corporations with subtle shades of investment potential. How do you select a handful from among all of them? How do you achieve true diversification? How can the fundamentals help you to cut through the volumes of available information and simplify the decision? These are some of the questions this book is designed to answer. The tools of fundamental analysis can and should help you to narrow down your list of choices to a few important indicators. No one can reasonably be expected to study dozens of indicators and to then be able to make a sound selection. The key to making the decision is based on *your* personal risk standards and identification of a few key but revealing indicators.

This book is not just an introduction to a range of analytical tools collectively called *fundamental analysis*—it is more. It is designed to help you put those tools to work in identifying risk levels, making valid and reliable comparisons, and ultimately in picking stocks for your portfolio. It is this activity—deciding which stocks to buy, how long to hold them, and when to sell—that lies at the center of every investment program. Even if you pick the stock of well-managed, financially sound companies, if your timing is off, your profits will not be at the pace you would hope and expect. Fundamental analysis helps you to quantify value and financial strength; of equal importance, it helps you to time your decisions to maximize the potential for profits in your stock selection.

With this in mind, you need the numbers as a starting point, the information you find in corporate audited financial statements and their footnotes, which includes quarterly filing papers and annual statements. Beyond these sources, you need to know how to read financial news and apply new information to a stock's value; how to anticipate economic changes in the broad market; and how those changes are likely to affect stocks; and how to identify a company's position within its industry and sector.

This book, part of the Getting Started In series, provides basic information on the complex topic of fundamental analysis in a way intended to help anyone go through the concepts and definitions without trouble. The combined visual and learning tools—the many practical examples, definitions in context, key points, checklists, and graphics—take vague concepts and put them into real-world action in a way that relates to the same decisions you face as an investor every day.

Financial Statements and What They Reveal

The universal regard for money is the one hopeful fact in our civilization.

—George Bernard Shaw, *Major Barbara*, 1905

You are faced with a daunting task whenever you attempt to tackle a large body of information and digest it all at once. Advice to the overwhelmed: Begin at the beginning, proceed through to the end, and then stop. This explains why books are organized in chapters. An example of a very big body of information is *fundamental analysis* because it is broad, complex, and encompasses many different principles. This chapter "begins at the beginning" by looking at the best-known type of fundamental analysis, the financial statements.

For many analysts, the fundamentals are limited to a study of just the numbers. But if you confine your study and comparisons to the financial statements, then the study itself is flawed. Using financial statements as a starting point in a wider program of fundamental analysis, the broader study includes much more. In the post-Enron age, you need to be less trusting of even the audited financial statement; you need more than just the word of the company and its auditors to ensure that the conclusions you reach are based on *valid* information.

Financial Statements: A Starting Point

The financial statement is a starting point, in many respects. Often considered the most important form of what are broadly called the

---

Key Point

The financial statements are a *starting point* in analysis. They are most useful when they highlight questions you need to ask to get more details.

---

fundamental analysis

the study of a company's financial strength, based on historical data; sector and industry position; management; dividend history; capitalization; and the potential for future growth. The combination of historical information and fiscal status collectively represent all data not directly related to the price of stock, and this body of information is used to define value investing and to compare one stock to another.

ratio

an analytical expression of relationships between values, expressed in fractional or percentage form. The ratio clarifies numerical relationships and makes trend analysis easier to manage and understand.

"fundamentals," the formal statements are a centerpiece and anyone embarking on the selection of stocks needs to be able to read these statements. They cannot, however, be used exclusively. They give you a place to begin checking and judging the financial results. The statements also provide an investigative starting point to confirm an existing trend, or to show a deviation from that trend, or even to launch further searches. In other words, fundamental analysis should not be limited to a passive view of recent historical reports; it is the starting point for a dynamic investigation of the fiscal validity in what you are being told. (Chapters 3 and 5 examine aspects of this all-important question in greater detail.)

Analysts use a series of tools to make judgments about financial statements and the numbers they contain. The *ratio* is a valuable shorthand tool used to track financial trends and to summarize a report. It is valuable because it aids in comprehension. For example, "3 to 1" is easily comprehended, whereas "$40,494 to $13,498" is more difficult to grasp.

Ratios are explored in considerable details in Chapters 7 and 8. In fact, beyond the study of financial statements, effective use of ratios helps translate the numbers into useful analytical conclusions. The ratio is used to track information as part of a trend. It is not enough to try and draw conclusions from just looking at the numbers as they are reported this quarter or this year; to truly understand what is going on with a company, you want to look at the longer view, the *trend*. A trend shows what was going on yesterday, what is going on today and—when properly studied—what is likely to go on tomorrow.

Thinking for a moment about how trends work, you come to realize that the use of these data in trend form is quite powerful. For example, a company may have reported ever-growing sales and profits over many years. Naturally, there comes a point where an established trend of annual growth cannot be sustained; the trend gradually flattens out; its rate of acceleration decreases; and sales and profits both "settle down" to a slower pace. This is not bad news, necessarily. In fact, trends do tend to even out over time as a statistical reality. If the company maintains related ratio-based aspects (such as a ceiling on expenses, for example) it is a sign that the growth curve, while slowing down, is being managed well by the company. On the other hand, if the sales levels begin to drop, but expenses keep rising, it means the company is heading for trouble.

trend

a long-term tendency reflected in how a corporation's financial results change over time; how related accounts emerge as status changes; and how a previously established pattern of growth begins, often gradually, to change.

In this situation it would not be revealing to simply look at the latest results from operations and draw conclusions. You need the larger long-term trend to understand what the latest numbers reveal. Without the trend, your analysis would be severely limited. This is what is meant by the use of the financial statements as a starting point, while also relying on much more.

The trend is also going to be revealing when managed through statistical tools. In the following section, some of these tools are explained in greater detail. Averaging of information over time is necessary because it is difficult to appreciate a trend in the moment. Moving averages are necessary to smooth out results. While many analysts do not like to admit it, financial results are chaotic. If you look at the immediate moment in terms of a company's sales, costs, expenses and profits, you see a lot of inconsistency; widely diverse reported results; and temporary aberrations from month to month. Even a full year's report is going to represent an averaging of 12 months' reports. This averaging absorbs cyclical changes from one season to the next; unusual activity (above or below the average) caused by numerous unforeseen events; and even unexplained changes due to accounting timing problems, monthly cycles, and even customer-based payments or order placement. The immediate trend is largely chaotic and impossible to read. This is why you need to base analysis on a variety of averaging devices. The moving average is the most reliable among these because it smoothes out the chaos of what you see and read today.

Moving Averages—In Various Forms

An examination of reported results is always difficult to interpret when you look only at the raw data. Look at sales trends as an example. A particular company's reported results show that sales have been increasing at the rate of 12 to 15 percent every year over the past five years. Costs have remained consistently at around 59 percent of sales; and expenses have risen only slightly over the period. Thus, net profits have come in at around 4 percent each and every year. Table 1.1 shows a summary with the most recent years shown last.

Key Point
Moving averages reveal critical information. For example, if sales are rising but profits are falling—or worse, the company is reporting losses—that is a sign of poor management.

The sales, costs, expenses, and profit trend summarized here is one of the most valuable analyses you can perform. It displays a positive trend of ever-growing sales *and* increased dollar amount of profits, maintenance of cost, and expense and profit relationships to sales—which is a sign of a well-planned fiscal program—and perhaps most important of all, keeping expenses in check relative to the other numerical values.

TABLE 1.1 Sales Trends for One Company (in millions)			
Year	Sales	Costs	Expenses	Profits
1	$4,775	$2,788	$1,796	$191
2	5,365	3,176	1,970	219
3	6,159	3,609	2,301	249
4	6,922	4,112	2,507	303
5	7,857	4,612	2,946	299

By the same argument, it is likely that a poorly managed company will experience deterioration of these relations specifically during periods of growth. Thus, costs rise as a percentage of sales; the dollar amount of expenses exceeds the rate of increase in sales, and, as a direct consequence, net profits decline. It is quite common to see a company's sales rising while profits decline, and even lead to net losses.

Because these trends are not easily spotted in the moment (for example, from one quarterly financial statement to the next), moving averages are popularly used in all types of stock market analysis. Technicians like moving averages to track and predict stock price changes over time and to prepare and study price charts. However, fundamental analysis benefits equally well from employing the *moving average* in its various forms.

To understand the advanced variations of moving averages, we begin by demonstrating how the *simple moving average* works. It is a study of the average using a set number of values. For example, if we look a series of entries in a field, we can develop a simple moving average.

A field of several values over a period of time is shown next. This may be sales, net profits, expenses, or any other financial value that you might want to study as part of a program of fundamental analysis. These fields are numbered from the oldest (i.e., 1) to the most recent:

moving average
a statistical tool used by market analysts, involving the use of a field of values over time. The moving average employs a specific number of field values and as a new value is added, an older one is dropped off.

simple moving average
the most basic variation of the moving average. A field of the most recent values is averaged and, as each new value is entered, the oldest value is dropped off so that the number of values studied remains constant.

Number	Value	Number	Value
1	427	6	1,113
2	833	7	800
3	619	8	634
4	211	9	1,005
5	952	10	716

The first aspect of this field worth mentioning is that the range is quite wide. With 10 different entries, it would be quite impossible to anticipate the next entry in this field, because it varies so much. However, if you follow a moving average, you will gain a less volatile view of what is occurring in this trend. To compute a moving average, add up the values and then divide by the number of values.

Formula: Simple Moving Average

$$\frac{N_1 + N_2 + \ldots N_n}{T} = A$$

where

  N = numerical; values in the field

  T = total number of values

  A = simple moving average

A simple moving average of the five most recent fields would show how averaging smoothes out even the most volatile trend:

Fields in Average	Calculation	Average
1–5	(427 + 833 + 619 + 211 + 952) ÷ 5	608
2–6	(833 + 619 + 211 + 952 + 1,113) ÷ 5	746
3–7	(619 + 211 + 952 + 1,113 + 800) ÷ 5	739
4–8	(211 + 952 + 1,113 + 800 + 634) ÷ 5	742
5–9	(952 + 1,113 + 800 + 634 + 1,005) ÷ 5	901
6–10	(1,113 + 800 + 634 + 1,005 + 716) ÷ 5	854

weighted moving average

a variation of moving average in which greater influence is given to more recent field values and less to older field values.

Figure 1.1 shows the range of all 10 fields *and* the moving average in this example. Note that the values in the field are quite volatile; but the moving average reduces that volatility, so that tracking the trend over time is made easier. This makes it easier for you to see the general direction of the trend over time.

Some variations on the moving average include the *weighted moving average* and the *exponential moving average*. You may consider the latest information to be more important than older information, so more recent values may be weighted, for example.

Example of a Weighted Moving Average

You are studying a field of five values, as in the previous example. You want to weight the average so that the latest value has twice the influence on the moving average; so you count each field once in a five-part average, but you double the most recent field. The total is then divided by six:

> **exponential moving average**
> a type of weighted moving average, the formula for which gives greater weight to the most recent field value, while accumulating the overall average by adding the latest value to the existing field.

Fields in Average	Calculation	Average
1–5	$(427 + 833 + 619 + 211 + 952 + 952) \div 6$	666
2–6	$(833 + 619 + 211 + 952 + 1{,}113 + 1{,}113) \div 6$	807
3–7	$(619 + 211 + 952 + 1{,}113 + 800 + 800) \div 6$	749
4–8	$(211 + 952 + 1{,}113 + 800 + 634 + 634) \div 6$	724
5–9	$(952 + 1{,}113 + 800 + 634 + 1{,}005 + 1{,}005) \div 6$	918
6–10	$(1{,}113 + 800 + 634 + 1{,}005 + 716 + 716) \div 6$	831

These recalculated moving average results change the outcome slightly when compared to the previous moving average. The distinction may appear minor, but it becomes important when it involves financial information, where most recent field importance can be a significant factor.

The exponential moving average is an example of a mathematical process that is often made more complicated in its explanation than it needs to be. It is simply a formulated moving average. It begins by calculating an exponent (or multiplier). For example, if you are calculating a moving average for a field of five values, you divide 2 by the number of values—or 5:

$$2 \div 5 = 0.4$$

Next, you calculate the simply moving average for the first five periods. Returning to the previous example:

$$(427 + 833 + 619 + 211 + 952) \div 5 = 608$$

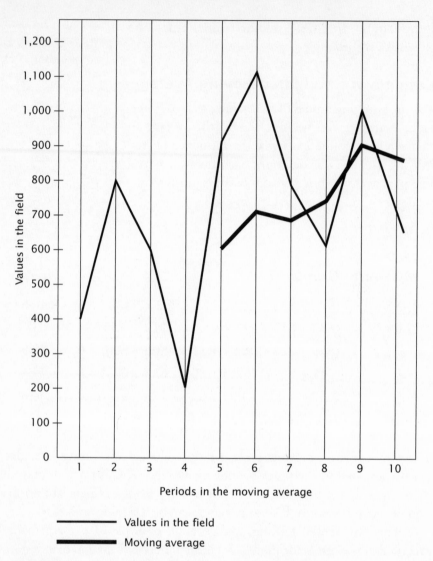

Periods in the moving average

———— Values in the field

━━━━ Moving average

FIGURE 1.1 Range of All 10 Fields and Moving Average

The moving average is then subtracted from the next occurring field value (number 6):

$$1113 - 608 = 505$$

This remainder is multiplied by the exponent:

$$505 \times 0.4 = 202$$

This value is then added to the previous moving average (or, if negative, subtracted from it) to arrive at the sixth period's exponential moving average:

$$202 + 608 = 810$$

This process is carried through for each subsequent field:

Field	Previous Value	New Average	New Difference	Exponent	Value	Average
1–5	0.4	608	608			
6	1,113	608	505	0.4	202	810
7	800	810	−10	0.4	−4	806
8	634	806	−172	0.4	−69	737
9	1,005	737	268	0.4	107	844
10	716	844	−128	0.4	−51	793

The calculation of various types of moving averages may be programmed into a spreadsheet program such as Microsoft Excel; in that case you would need to only enter the latest field value to arrive at a new moving average. However, simplicity is often the best outcome to strive for and, if the results of a more complex calculation are not much different than an easier one, it makes sense to go with the easier one.

Key Point

When two different methods of calculating moving average produce little change in the outcome, go with the easier method. It saves time, reduces the chance for error, and is more easily comprehended.

The essential value of using moving averages is to remove volatility from an existing trend, so that its direction is more easily recognizable. One final statistical rule of thumb is to remove exceptionally big changes from a field of study when they are not typical. For example, if a field of outcomes over a period of quarters is generally within a narrow range, and one quarter's results are exceptionally high or low, you may want to exclude the exception, recognizing that it distorts the more "normal" range of outcomes. You should remove these spikes under the following guidelines:

1. The spike is far outside the normal range of outcomes.

2. The change is untypical of fields before and after. The range of results returns to a previously established level.

3. The causes of the spike are nonrecurring and do not represent an adjustment of previously reported results. (For example, if profits are reported far below the average because previous outcomes were incorrect, do not remove the spike. But if a one-time loss is reported due to a natural disaster, it should be removed because it is nonrecurring.)

Using averaging as a method for managing information makes sense. Financial statements, consisting of dollar values, are difficult to interpret. Averaging of data, combined with the use of ratios, help to make a trend recognizable and plain; this is far preferable to trying to make sense of columns of numbers. The financial statements, expressed in dollars, are difficult to interpret without applying these tools. In fact, you should never look at a single set of statements to draw conclusions about a corporation's capital strength or operating results; all fundamental analysis should be studied as part of a larger trend over time. Of course, to begin, you will need to understand the purpose of each of the three major financial statements. The next section explains these in detail.

Balance Sheet

The first of three financial statements is the *balance sheet*. This statement summarizes everything the

balance sheet

one of three financial statements, reporting values of assets, liabilities, and net worth as of a specific date; that date is the ending date of a quarter or year. The total of assets (properties) is equal to the sum of liabilities (debts) and net worth (equity of the company).

company owns and everything it owes to others, as well as its financial value.

This statement is called a "balance sheet" for two reasons. First of all, it is a summary of the balances in all asset, liability, and net worth accounts as of a specific date. Second, the various sections are balanced to one another; the total of all assets is always equal to the sum of all liability and net worth accounts.

The properties of the company, its *assets*, constitute the first part of the balance sheet.

Assets fall into several subgroups and later on, when it comes time to look at specific ratios of the balance sheet, these subgroups will make sense. They are arranged to classify assets according to their attributes and degree of *liquidity*. This is a critical distinction. So one set of assets is highly liquid (cash and assets that can be converted to cash within one year) and other assets are not liquid at all (such as equipment and real estate, for example).

The most common subgroups of assets are described in the following list:

- *Current assets* exist in the form of cash or as assets that can be converted to cash within 12 months (accounts receivable, notes receivable, marketable securities, and inventory, for example)

- *Long-term assets,* which are also called "fixed" assets, include any *capital assets* that cannot be deducted in the year purchased but must be depreciated over several years. These are shown on the balance sheet at purchase price, minus *accumulated depreciation*.

- *Deferred assets* and *prepaid assets* are special classes of assets. These categories are used to manage timing differences. For example, if a company pays for merchandise this year, but that cost belongs in the following year, it would be improper to report that as a cost for this year; it would

assets
the properties owned by a company, listed on the balance sheet in dollar value and making up the first of three sections on the balance sheet.

liquidity
an attribute of an asset relating to its convertibility to cash. Some assets can be quickly and easily converted to cash and are considered highly liquid; other assets cannot be easily or quickly converted, and those assets have low liquidity.

current assets
those assets in the form of cash or that are convertible to cash within 12 months, including accounts and notes receivable, marketable securities, and inventory.

long-term assets

also called "fixed" assets, are the purchased value of assets that cannot be deducted in the year purchased but must be depreciated over time. On the balance sheet, long-term assets are reported at purchase price minus accumulated depreciation.

capital assets

expenditures that are required by tax law to be capitalized (reported as assets on the balance sheet) rather than written off as current-year expenses in the year purchased. These are reported at net value (purchase price minus accumulated depreciation).

distort the numbers. So instead of recognizing this cost in the current year, the payment is set up as a deferred asset. In the following year it is reversed and recorded in the applicable period.

Prepaid assets are similar. In some instances a corporation pays an expense that extends over more than one year, so the portion applying to the future is set up as a prepaid asset. For example, a three-year insurance premium may be paid in advance; the current portion is recorded as an expense but the remainder is placed in the "prepaid assets" account and amortized over the period to which the expense applies.

- *Intangible assets* are assets without physical value. This is perhaps the most difficult class of assets to understand. Typical are accounts such as goodwill—that is, the value of reputation and brand-name recognition often assigned a value at the time a company or division is originally bought—and other nontangible assets such as certain kinds of contractual matters. A "covenant not to compete" is a contract in which one company promises to not open competing outlets for a specified period of time after a sale; this would be recorded as an intangible asset. It provides value to the purchasing company, but there is no physical asset.

The second section of the balance sheet is used for recording liabilities. There are usually two major sections:

- *Current liabilities* are those payable within one year. In this group companies include accounts payable, taxes payable, and the next 12 months' obligation for payments on all notes and contracts.

The distinction between current and long-term is crucial to many balance sheet ratios.

- *Long-term liabilities* include all debts that are payable beyond the next 12 months. These include long-term lease payments (except the current portion), note or loan payments due after the next 12 months, bond repayments, and other recorded debts of the company.

- *Deferred credits*, a third category, is included with liabilities. While these are not technically debts, they are listed in this section of the balance sheet. Normally these are sales receipts received in the current year yet belonging in the following year. It would distort the operating results to simply report these as sales, so they are classified as deferred credits. Next year, the deferred credit is removed and the credit is recorded as a sale.

accumulated depreciation
the value of all depreciation claimed on fixed assets from the date of purchase through the latest balance sheet date. Long-term assets are reported at purchase price minus accumulated depreciation and remain on the balance sheet until those assets are sold. Eventually, fully depreciated assets will report a net value of zero—once the full purchase price has been completely depreciated. At that point, the accumulated depreciation will be equal to the purchase price of the asset.

The third and final section of the balance sheet records the company's *net worth*, also called *stockholders' equity*. The way that the double-entry bookkeeping system records transactions—with everything involving a debit and a credit—the balance sheet always ties the three sections together in a basic formula:

$$\text{Assets} - \text{Liabilities} = \text{Net worth}$$

On the form itself, there are two major sections. Assets are reported on the top; and liabilities plus net worth are reported below. The sum of these two sections is always exactly the same.

deferred assets

the value of costs and expenses paid currently but applying to a future period. Those payments are deferred so that they can be booked as costs or expenses in the future. In the following year or years, the deferred asset is reduced and the applicable amount transferred to the income statement.

prepaid assets

the net value of expenses paid this year when all or part applies to the future. In the applicable period, a portion of the prepaid asset is reduced and recorded as an expense, so that it is recognized in the correct reporting year.

Within the net worth section, several specific classifications are going to be found. Many complex subaccounts may be found for multiple classes of stock and other items such as dividends and taxes payable. The primary segments of the equity section include:

- *Capital stock* is the original issued value of stock, which may include several different classes. Common stock, preferred stock, and multiple issues might be involved. As the original issue value, capital stock's current value is not adjusted; it remains on the books at its initial value. For example, if a corporation issued one million shares at $10 per share, then the capital stock value in this section will also be reported at $10 million, even if current market value is much higher.

- *Retained earning* is the accumulated net value of reported profits and losses over a company's entire history. Each year's profit is added to retained earnings (or losses subtracted).

- *Profit or loss* is the current year's net profit; this amount will tie to the reported net profit on the operating statement.

The organization of the balance sheet is uniform in format. This format is summarized in Figure 1.2.

Statement of Operations

The balance sheet summarizes account balances and values as of a specific date, usually the end of the quarter or fiscal year. The *statement of operations*, in comparison, summarizes a series of transactions over a period of time (a year or a quarter, normally), with the ending date identical to the date of the balance sheet. So the balance sheet reports balances

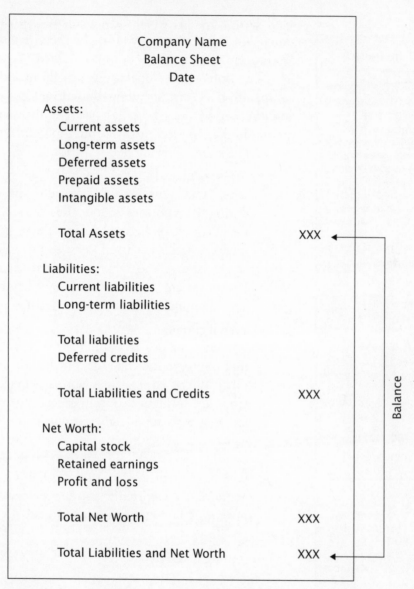

Company Name
Balance Sheet
Date

Assets:
　Current assets
　Long-term assets
　Deferred assets
　Prepaid assets
　Intangible assets

　Total Assets　　　　　　　　　　XXX

Liabilities:
　Current liabilities
　Long-term liabilities

　Total liabilities
　Deferred credits

　Total Liabilities and Credits　　　XXX

Net Worth:
　Capital stock
　Retained earnings
　Profit and loss

　Total Net Worth　　　　　　　　XXX

　Total Liabilities and Net Worth　　XXX

Balance

FIGURE 1.2　Organization of the Balance Sheet

intangible assets

the recorded value of assets that have no physical existence, such as goodwill or incomplete agreements. These are recorded along with other assets, but these would be excluded from the calculation of *tangible* book value of a company.

current liabilities

all of the debts of a company that are payable within the next 12 months, including accounts and taxes payable, lease payments, and payments on loans and notes.

long-term liabilities

all debts of a company extended beyond the next 12 months, including payments on contracts, notes and loans; bonds; and other liabilities not due within the coming 12 months.

as of December 31, while the statement of operations summarizes activity for the year *ending* December 31.

The statement of operations usually includes comparative reports including the current period and the period preceding (last year or the same quarter in the last year). It runs from top to bottom and includes the following major sections:

- *Revenues* may also be called "sales" or "gross sales." This is the amount received or earned during the reporting period. (Revenues normally consist of a combination of cash payments as well as charged sales; so this value is not always the same as cash receipts.) Revenues are also reduced by "returns and allowances" or "discounts granted" to customers.

- *Cost of goods sold* is a summary of changes in inventory; merchandise purchased; and other "direct" costs such as labor and freight. Costs are distinguished from expenses by the fact that costs are directly attributable to the generation of revenues. The percentage of cost of goods sold is expected to remain fairly consistent as sales rise and fall. Costs are normally reported to capture changes in inventory, along the following format:

Beginning inventory	XXXXX
Plus: Merchandise purchased	XXXXX
Plus: Direct labor	XXXXX
Plus: Other direct costs	XXXXX
Subtotal	XXXXX
Minus: Ending inventory	XXXXX
Net Cost of goods sold	XXXXX

The cost of goods sold is deducted from revenues to arrive at *gross profit*, which may also be described as profit before expenses.

- *Expenses* is often subdivided between "selling" and "general and administrative" (overhead) expense classifications. These are amounts spent or obligated that are not directly tied to generation of revenues. As a general rule, analysts expect expenses to remain within a relatively narrow range even as revenues rise. Increased dollar value of profits is the result when costs remain consistent in relation to sales; and when expenses are held in check.

- *Net operating profit or loss* is the difference between gross profit and expenses. The "operating" profit or loss is distinguished from the true *net* profit or loss, which takes other, nonoperational income or expenses into account (see below).

- *Other income and expense* will include all nonoperating adjustments to operating profit or loss. These include profit or loss from currency exchange; interest income or expense; and federal tax liabilities, for example. The net operating profit is increased or decreased for the net difference between "other" income and expense.

- *Net profit or loss* is the "bottom line," the net remaining when other income and expense is deducted from the operating profit or loss.

A summary of the statement of operations is shown in Figure 1.3

deferred credits

sales and other credits received in advance of the applicable reporting period, recorded in the liability section of the balance sheet pending transfer in the future to the operating statement.

net worth

the value of a corporation; the difference between assets and liabilities, consisting of capital stock, retained earnings, current profit or loss; and minus obligation for dividend payments.

shareholders' equity

(also called *stockholders' equity*) the net worth of a company, consisting of several accounts but essentially the net remaining after liabilities are subtracted from assets.

Company Name
Statement of Operations
For the period beginning _____ and ending _____

Revenues   XXX

Cost of Goods Sold:
        Beginning inventory
        Plus: Merchandise
        Plus: Direct labor
        Plus: Other direct costs
            Subtotal
            Less: Ending inventory

Less: Cost of Goods Sold   XXX

Gross Profit   XXX

Less: Expenses   XXX

Operating Profit or Loss   XXX

Other Income or Expense   XXX

Net Profit or Loss   XXX

FIGURE 1.3   Statement of Operations

Statement of Cash Flows

The third of the three major financial statements is the *statement of cash flows*. This is the least understood of the three statements. It reports on the inflow and outflow of cash over a specified period of time (that period is identical to the reporting period of the statement of operations).

The statement has two distinct sections. First is a detailed summary of the cash-based transactions for the year, including "sources" of funds, "applications" of funds, and the net increase or decrease for the period. By "cash-based," this means the line items make adjustments to remove all noncash entries. For example, depreciation is a noncash expense prepared by way of journal entry. A debit is entered on the statement of operations as an expense, and an offsetting credit is entered in the balance sheet under "long-term assets," where the gross value of capital assets is reduced. On the statement of cash flows, the first two lines of this section are usually involved with net profits and adjustments for noncash expenses (like depreciation). The "sources of funds" section may further include other sources, such as proceeds from the sale of capital assets, income from selling an operating unit or subsidiary, payments received for an issue of corporate bonds or proceeds from new loans. A simplified summary of sources of funds (the column heading $000 indicates that reported totals are shown in millions of dollars):

capital stock
the reported issue value of all outstanding stock at original value, shown as the first item in a corporation's net worth section of the balance sheet.

retained earnings
the accumulated net profits or losses a company has reported over its history; profits are added and losses are subtracted, from the previous year's net retained earnings.

profit or loss
the net reported annual profits earned by a corporation. The reported net profit or loss on the operating statement also appears as a single item on the net worth section of the corporation's balance sheet and, upon closing the books for the year, net profit or loss is added to the accumulated retained earnings.

Sources of Funds ($000)

Net profit	$13,466
Plus: noncash expenses included above	1,044
Proceeds from the sale of capital assets	6,440
Receipts from the sale of subsidiary companies	3,050
Newly issued bond proceeds	4,000
Proceeds, newly acquired notes and loans	550
Total sources of funds	$28,550

Applications (payments) of funds may also involve numerous sources, including the cost to acquire capital assets, payments for acquisitions of new companies, retirement of a bond issue, repayment of loans and notes, dividends paid, and decreases in other long-term liabilities (increases in long-term liabilities would be reported as a source of funds). For example:

Applications of Funds ($000)

Acquisition of capital assets	$ 8,065
Paid for acquisition of new subsidiaries	2,882
Retirement of existing bond issue	5,000
Repayment of loans and notes	338
Dividends paid to shareholders	4,007
Decreases in long-term liabilities	884
Total applications of funds	$21,176

A final line follows these two sections, summarizing the net increase or decrease in funds for the period:

Net increase in funds	$7,374

The first section includes these detailed explanations, essentially revealing (1) where cash came
from and (2) where it was spent. In this example,
the corporation increased funds for the year by
$7.374 billion. (Remember, the $000 tells you that
the last section is excluded and the financial statement reports in millions of dollars.)

The second section of the statement of cash
flows summarizes the changes in current assets and
current liabilities for the period. The definition of the
difference between these current accounts is *working
capital*, and this is used to study the effectiveness of a
corporation's use of its money. The net changes in
current assets and liabilities will always equal the net
increase or decrease in funds reported in the first section. To those not familiar with double-entry bookkeeping, this is a mystery. But it really is not that
complex to understand. Because all transactions in-
volve equal value of debits and credits, the statement of cash flows is simply
a division between accounts. In the first section, sources and applications of
funds involve all noncurrent assets and liabilities and changes in net worth
(which also includes the current-year net profit or loss). The second section
shows changes in everything else as shown in Table 1.2.

**cost of
goods sold**
the section on the
statement of
operations follow-
ing reported rev-
enues. Cost of
goods sold con-
sists of changes in
inventory levels;
merchandise pur-
chased; direct
labor; and other
costs attributable
directly to generat-
ing revenues. The
cost of goods sold
is deducted from
sales to arrive at
gross profit.

**TABLE 1.2   Working Capital Changes Section in a Statement
of Cash Flow (in millions)**

	Changes in Working Capital ($000)		
	Jan 1	Dec. 31	Change
Cash	$ 6,442	$ 7,200	$ 758
Accounts Receivable	14,637	19,462	4,825
Notes Receivable	2,000	2,000	0
Marketable Securities	12,838	12,235	(603)
Inventory	7,112	8,440	1,328
Accounts Payable	(6,729)	(5,117)	1,612
Notes Payable	(618)	(702)	(84)
Taxes Payable	(5,580)	(6,042)	(462)
Net Working Capital	$30,102	$37,476	$7,374

Company Name
Statement of Cash Flows
For the period beginning _____ and ending _____

Sources of Funds:
Net profits
Noncash expenses
Proceeds from sales
Proceeds from loans
Other sources

Total Sources of Funds   XXX ◄

Applications of Funds:
Acquisition of capital assets
Acquisition of subsidiaries
Retirement of debts
Other applications

Total Applications of Funds   XXX

Net Increase or Decrease in Funds   XXX

Working Capital Change:

Current assets and liabilities,
beginning of period   XXX

Current assets and liabilities,
end of period   XXX

Net Change in Working Capital   XXX ◄

Balance

FIGURE 1.4 Statement of Cash Flows

The sections and organization of the statement of cash flows is summarized in Figure 1.4.

Comparative Financial Statements

In the beginning of this chapter, the importance of taking a broad view was emphasized. You cannot look at a single financial statement and judge a company's strength on that basis. Instead, you need to look at long-term trends, well designed analytical ratio-based programs, and to develop a series of tests. These quantify capital strength, working capital, internal controls, and profits, among other fundamental attributes.

The financial statement itself is rarely prepared as a stand-alone, isolated document. It is invariably prepared as a *comparative statement*, letting you look at today's results next to other, past results as well.

> **Key Point**
>
> Analysis is most valuable when it allows you to look at comparative information over time. Long-term trends are the key to discovering what is going on, but a single current statement by itself does not reveal much.

Comparisons are made on several bases, including:

1. *Year-to-year.* The most popular and best-known comparative financial statement is one that compares the most recent full year, to the year before. As with all comparative financial statements, any treatment of income, costs, or expenses that has changed requires a revision to past statements. This places all reported periods on the same premise; without this restated basis, a comparative statement would be misleading.

gross profit
the net difference between revenues and direct costs, or profit before expenses. It is a line item on the statement of operations following direct costs and preceding general and administrative expenses.

expenses
the grouping of spending reported on the statement of operations, for obligations not directly tied to generation of revenues. These include both selling expenses and general and administrative expenses and are the focus of internal controls, especially during periods of rapid sales expansion.

net operating profit or loss
the net remaining when expenses are deducted from gross profit, representing profit or loss from operations but excluding nonoperating income or expenses.

other income or expense

the adjustments made to operating profit or loss for nonoperating items, including currency exchange, interest income and expense, and income tax liabilities. The operating profit or loss is adjusted for the net difference, resulting in overall net profit.

net profit or loss

the net sum of operating profit or loss adjusted for other income and expense. It is the reported net amount that will be added to or subtracted from retained earnings and carried forward on the permanent books of the corporation.

2. *Quarter-to-quarter.* When a financial statement is prepared during the year, a comparative basis would involve comparisons on two formats: Current quarter to year-to-date is a popular method. A second is current quarter's year-to-date results compared to the same period in the past year.

3. *Long-term summary, key financial results.* Often seen in annual reports, the five-year or longer financial summary may be quite detailed. However, it is more likely to report key ingredients. These include gross sales, cost of goods sold, expenses, and profits. In addition, the long-term comparative summary may also show *earnings per share* (EPS) each year, dividends declared and paid, and other specialized information. (For example, if the corporation is primarily involved in retail sales, yearly information may show the number of stores opened or closed and even the year-end total number of retail sales space expressed in square feet.)

4. *Division-to-division.* A diversified company may be expected to be involved in numerous related or unrelated business ventures. When this occurs, it is difficult to judge the results of each division when a *consolidated statement* is all that is offered. With this in mind, some diversified corporations provide breakdowns and comparative statements for its major divisions. For example, in the case of Altria Corporation (symbol *MO*, also known as Philip Morris), a program of fundamental analysis would want to study separately the revenues and profits for domestic tobacco, international tobacco, and

the food division (Kraft Foods and more). All of these divisions have dissimilar attributes, and the trends in each should be analyzed separately. The consolidated results are far less revealing because specific trends are difficult to spot.

Footnotes

A major complaint made by stockholders—notably those without an accounting education—is that financial statements are too complex to understand. Indeed, most of the valuable information you need to perform in-depth fundamental analysis is going to be found in the *footnotes* to the financial statements.

The financial statements are only three pages. But the footnotes can expand the financial statement to over 100 pages in especially complicated situations. These are not easy to read or to comprehend. However, key explanations and disclosures may be found there. The most sensible way to deal with the high volume of complex material is to limit your search. Once you decide on a short list of what you consider important financial analyses you should perform, you can reduce the footnote-reading task to only a few pages.

For example, if you decide to analyze only five or six features of the financial statement and use less than 10 ratios, you can find verifying information within the footnotes, and scan for these selectively. It is rarely necessary to read all of the footnotes, so the problems come down to the question: Which of the footnotes must you read?

statement of cash flows
the financial statement used to summarize the movement of cash in and out of a business over a period of time, also called the cash flow statement or statement of sources and applications of funds.

comparative statement
a financial statement that summarizes results from year to year, between the same quarter-ending of subsequent years, or in some other breakdown such as between divisions and operating units of a larger corporation.

consolidated statement
a type of financial statement including combined results from all subsidiaries, even those in dissimilar lines of business.

footnotes

a series of explanatory notes, often including detailed narrative and financial breakdowns, to disclose important information and to expand upon the summarized data provided in the financial statements. Footnotes exist for dozens of purposes and are included as part of a complete set of financial statements.

transparency

a concept in corporate management defining the desirability of making full disclosures to stockholders so that operations, financial results, and accounting decisions are made in the open; the idea that nothing should be hidden from the investor or stockholder.

By reducing the overall examination of financial data to only a few important tests, you solve the problem once and for all. Unless you are happy to undertake a graduate study of accounting and auditing, you will not enjoy tackling a book-length and highly technical set of disclosures, so you need to develop means for coping with these notes.

It should be the task of auditors and corporate management to achieve *transparency* in their reports to stockholders. Unfortunately, little sincere effort has been put forth on the part of corporate management and auditing firms to provide stockholders with all of the information they need. In fact, the accounting rules in the United States are so complex that it is possible to manipulate the numbers to achieve a desired result without committing any outright fraud. The rules allow liberal interpretations and decisions that have important impact on the financial statement, while often leaving out important information as well.

This is where the value of fundamental analysis becomes so crucial. Even when corporations manipulate their results to make outcomes look as favorable as possible (and even when auditors cooperate with management in this practice), you can apply a limited number of financial ratios and track a few key trends. These allow you to follow results for yourself and to spot the emerging changes over time that may not be readily apparent in a study of the financial statements. Fundamental analysis is not merely an exercise in accounting; it can be and should be a method you can use to make value judgments about the stock of a number of corporations; to use intelligent tests to narrow down your list; and to pick the timing for buying and for selling shares based on the financial results.

This chapter explained the basic tools of fundamental analysis and also showed how the major financial statements are organized; what they report; and how they can be used as a starting point in an expanded program. In the next chapter, the basic stock market theories are explained and compared. These are valuable to you in your program of fundamental analysis, even though these "valuation theories" are usually discussed in terms of *technical analysis*, which is a study of stock prices and trends.

Most people familiar with these theories will be surprised to hear that stock market theories are valuable in fundamental analysis. In fact, though, the most important developer of one of these—the *Dow Theory*—originally developed his ideas for application in the financial realm. While his theories are employed today to track prices, you will discover that the relationship between the fundamental and the technical is much closer than most people believe. These theories are explored in depth in the next chapter.

technical analysis

a series of techniques employed to anticipate price movement in stocks; to study the causes and patterns of price and volume; and to anticipate the direction price is likely to move in the near future. Unlike fundamental analysis, which is rooted in financial reports of the corporation, technical analysis is primarily involved in prices and trends of a company's stock.

Basic Stock Market Theories

The new source of power is not money in the hands of a few but information in the hands of the many.
—John Naisbitt, *Megatrends*, 1984

When you read opinions, recommendations, and analysis by experts, you soon realize that there are a lot of people out there making suggestions—where to invest, how to invest, what to buy or sell, and why. Their reasoning is inconsistent, and for anyone looking in from the outside, the assumptions are, seemingly, never-ending.

For insiders, the range of theories about how to invest can be just as confusing. When it comes to money and power, you are likely to discover that there are as many opinions as there are people. But the range of opinions can be broken down into a few camps of thought—a handful of points of view concerning the market. This chapter explains and compares these major views about:

- Types of analysis.
- Market valuation theories.
- Various types of trends and their value.
- The kinds of investors and how they act within the market.
- The relationship between risk and profit.

These are essential basics for anyone embarking on a program of analysis within the market. All too often, new investors are thrown into the mix without being provided a broad view of how the market works (or at least, how various people *think* the market works). As a consequence, these newcomers are assaulted with various conclusions about the market without being told how or why those ideas have value.

Comparisons between Fundamental and Technical Analysis

If you listen to anyone debate the fundamentals versus the technical, you quickly realize that there is a lot of passion in both schools of thought. The fundamental investor believes in the numbers and assumes that future value can be identified by watching financial trends. In contrast, the technician is more interested in tracking a stock's price and in trying to anticipate the price trend.

The debate between these two theories is interesting because they are so far apart in basic assumptions. It is often the case in debates that each side shares some common ground, but disagrees on the essentials. As far as analysis goes, the fundamental and technical adherents have virtually nothing in common. The whole premise by which they pick stocks, decide when to sell, and establish value, is completely different on each side.

Key Point

Fundamental and technical analysis are not just two different approaches to the *same* question. They are entirely different in nature. Fundamentals deal with corporate financial results, while technical indicators focus on stock price trends.

The arguments against the other side may define the differences as well as any other point. Fundamental analysts proclaim that financial results are the only dependable means for establishing the value of a company. The price trends, in the fundamental view, are short term, chaotic, and unreliable, caused by many conflicting and inaccurate momentary factors. The immediate supply and demand within the market is illogical, price movement overreacts to news and gossip, and much of the daily price movement is either random or artificial. These points are convincing.

Technicians have an equally convincing argument. They point out that by the time you obtain accurate and reliable information, it is woefully out of date. The historical financial information published by a company has nothing to do with today's pricing trends or with the direction of price movement, the technician believes. Ultimately, it is the timing of decisions that determines whether you earn a profit or suffer a loss in the market.

Which side is right? In this book a detailed examination of fundamental analysis is provided with examples, definitions, and graphics. For now an objective analysis of the essential technical tools is worthwhile. Every investor, even the faithful fundamentalist, should be aware of the basics of the other side. Combining the essential tools of both fundamental and technical analysis may prove to be the most effective methodology for anyone.

Following are the brief concepts of technical analysis. (Remember, a detailed study of the technical side will involve more in-depth analysis and study; these are only the basics. For more study in this field, one of the best books on the topic is *Getting Started in Technical Analysis* by Jack D. Schwager).

chart
the basic tool of technical analysis, used to study price movements in the belief that specific patterns signal how future prices will change.

1. *Charts.* The *chart* is the essential tool of technical analysis. The technician believes that prices move to establish specific patterns and that a study of those patterns will indicate the price movements of the immediate future.

   The most popular and simplest type of chart is the *bar chart*. This is a series of vertical lines, one for each day. The line shows the range from high to low price during that day, and includes a small horizontal line moving to the right, showing the closing price. Some bar charts also include a small horizontal line moving to the left to indicate the day's opening price. A daily bar chart and its features are shown in Figure 2.1.

bar chart
a form of price charting in which a series of daily prices is shown side by side over time. The vertical bar shows the range of prices during the day from high to low. A small horizontal extension to the right shows the closing price for the day and some bar charts also include a small horizontal extension to the left for the day's opening price.

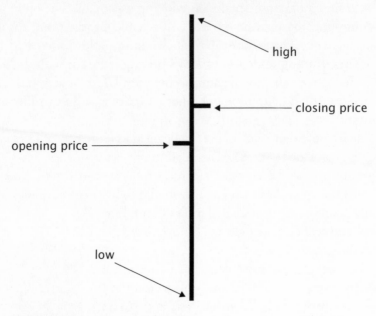

FIGURE 2.1   Daily Bar Chart

close-only chart

a price tracking chart showing closing price only, but not the range of high and low price ranges.

The *close-only chart* is a more summarized price tracking tool. It does not include high and low prices, but simply shows the closing price. Over an extended period of time, close-only charts may be augmented with a long-term moving average of the price as well.

The *point-and-figure chart* is more complex that the more common price charts. Ignoring the time element, the point-and-figure variety is made up of a running series of Xs and Os. Although calculation of the degree of movement affects how the chart is constructed, Xs represent upward trend and price movements, and Os are downward trends.

The *candlestick chart* is the most advanced form of price tracking. In the candlestick, the range between opening and closing prices (the "body") moves vertically, and if price moved above or below the body, additional lines (called "shadows") extend above and below. The direction of movement for the day is also indicated. When the closer is higher than the open price, the body is white; when the closer is lower, the body is black. These distinctions are summarized in Figure 2.2.

The importance of *price trends* in technical analysis is crucial. The entire system is based on the idea that the most recent trends reveal and anticipate what is going to happen next.

point-and-figure chart

a type of chart used by technicians to track price but not time. Rising prices and trends are represented by a series of Xs and the stronger the movement, the more Xs appear. Downward prices and trends are shown as a series of vertical Os.

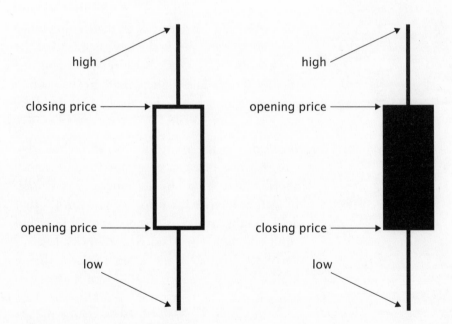

FIGURE 2.2 Candlestick Chart

candlestick chart
a form of chart that efficiently summarizes a day's trading range, high and low price, and direction of movement.

price trends
the tendencies of stock prices to behave in particular ways over time, and to demonstrate patterns that, in the view of the technical analyst, reveal how prices are going to move next.

trading range
the distance between a stock's established high and low prices over a period of time, representing the current levels of price supply and demand for the stock.

support
the lowest likely price for a stock within its established trading range.

2. *Trading range.* Charts are used to track prices and trends and to find specific patterns in a stock's movement, volatility, and direction. Technical analysis is based on a study of the patterns seen in charts and of the *trading range* they reveal. A stock's trading range is the distance between high and low prices, demonstrated over time. For example, if a stock has traded for the past three months between 28 and 34, it has a six-point trading range. This is significant because, until the prices moves above or below the trading range, it establishes the current supply and demand levels for that stock.

3. *Support and resistance.* Trading range is a defining aspect of price analysis. A stock is expected to remain within the trading range until a significant change occurs, brought on by news, events, earnings surprises, or shifting demand for shares. The lowest price in the trading range is called *support*, and is the lowest price that the stock is likely to trade within the established trading range. The highest price in the trading range is *resistance*, which is the highest price the stock is likely to trade.

4. *Breakout.* To the nontechnical, the whole discussion of trading range, support, and resistance appears interesting but not especially revealing. In fact, as long as the price remains within that defined range, there is not much to observe beyond enabling you to define a stock's level of volatility. A broad range is more volatile than a narrow one. However, trading range does become interesting when there is a *breakout*. This is a movement in price above or below the established range, usually indicating a change in the range itself, and creating a new trading pattern, different trading range, and perhaps a change in volatility as well.

5. *Trading patterns.* Remember, technical analysts look for specific patterns to reveal and anticipate future price movement, often as quickly as a matter of days or even hours. These patterns have been given names. These include *gaps* (patterns showing space between one day's close and another day's open); *spikes* (an unusually exaggerated price movement well above or below previously established trading levels); *triangles* (trading patterns establishing either a broadening of the price range over a series of days, or a narrowing); *flags* (short-term price congestion with trading range running parallel); *pennants* (short-term price congestion in which the trading lines converge); *V formations* (sudden price reversals, such as a new price high, followed by an immediate downward movement, or a sudden and sharp decline followed by a sharp price reversal); and *head and shoulders* (a popular three-part price trend in which three stages are experienced: stage numbers one and three establish a trading top or resistance level, and the middle stage sets a resistance at a higher level; a reverse head and shoulders has the same pattern, but involves support levels and establishment of bottom price levels).

resistance
the highest likely price for a stock within its established trading range.

breakout
a price movement above resistance or below support levels, which signals a change in trading range and volatility for a stock.

gaps
spaces between one day's close and another day's opening price.

spikes
exceptionally big changes in price, upward or downward, when compared to established trading levels; and characterized by a return to previous levels after the spike.

The Value of a Combined Method

The debate over which analytical method to use—fundamental or technical—is never-ending. Both systems provide useful and valuable information. For example, if you are a true-blue fundamental analyst, you will not want to ignore sudden and unexplained changes in a stock's price volatility. That may indicate important changes growing out of the fundamentals or, perhaps, anticipating

triangles

trading patterns in which the range of high-to-low prices broadens or narrows within a short period of time.

flags

short-term trading patterns in a specific direction in which the gap between high and low remains constant.

pennants

short-term trading patterns in a specific direction in which the gap between high and low converges over time.

V formations

a price pattern typified by a sharp increase or decrease in price to a new high or low level, followed immediately by a sharp reversal and price movement in the opposite direction.

fundamental changes. Trading ranges (and thus, price volatility) are related not only to short-term market news and gossip, but also to fundamental changes.

Key Point

Even though fundamental and technical philosophies don't agree, both are valuable. You gain important information by reviewing financial *and* price information, and using both to make decisions.

Rather than making the decision to use one method or another exclusively, it makes more sense to take useful intelligence from both sides and use them to confirm trends, to anticipate short-term changes, or to judge a stock based on various features.

Example

You are thinking about buying one of three stocks that are comparable on several fundamental measurements. These tests include dividend yield, P/E ratio, working capital, and operating trends (sales growth and net profits). You cannot decide which of these stocks would be lower risk based on the consistency in the fundamental indicators. However, when you begin to view the technical side, you discover that one stock has reasonably low price volatility and a long-established trading range. That range has been moving in a gradual but consistent upward trend for several years. However, the other two stocks show far higher volatility. One has had considerable change in its trading range over the past year, in both directions at different times. The other is so volatile that no trading range is discernable at all.

From this simplified study of the technical indicators, you may conclude that the first of the three stocks is the lowest risk of all. Of course, fundamental analysts will remind you that short-term trends are unreliable and, additionally, looking to historical price movement does not indicate what the future will hold. In other words, there are no guarantees that the assumptions you make about safety of an investment are always best guesses.

In the market, your best guess—based on using information from both fundamental and technical indicators—is far better than a mere guess. You will not be right 100 percent of the time, either in stock selection or in the timing of decisions to buy or sell. The purpose to analysis is to improve your averages. If you can be right more often than wrong, you are ahead of the average, and that is the real goal.

Because short-term price movements are random and chaotic (as you will see in the following sections of this chapter), you cannot use technical analysis exclusively to pick long-term investments.

head and shoulders

a price trend pattern involving three stages. In an upward head and shoulders pattern, stages one and three show prices reaching a resistance level before retreating, and the middle stage tracking the same movements but with a higher resistance level. In a downward head and shoulders pattern, the same stages exist, but they involve support levels rather than resistance.

In fact, that idea is contradictory and irrational. The nature of short-term movement has nothing to do with what may be called "value-based investing." This is a reference to the ideal of picking stocks likely to grow over the long term. A stock's price, whether today, yesterday, or in the future, has nothing to do with the value of the company as a long-term investment. This critical reality is so often overlooked by investors, but it is the key to understanding the value of each method, as well as to avoiding the common error of assuming that both methods provide equal information but in different ways.

Key Point

A stock's price has no direct connection to a company's financial results. The test methods are based on different assumptions, and provide entirely different types of market intelligence.

For example, a study of price trends may reveal trading range patterns and give you an advance signal of price movements that are going to occur over the next few days or even months. But what is that based on? Price reflects the market's level of supply and demand, and may have no relevance whatsoever to *value* itself. For example, if a large mutual fund decides to sell off its holdings of a company, thousands of shares are dumped on the market. That will cause a price decline because, unexpectedly, there is a large excess supply of shares. In the opposite scenario, that big mutual fund may decide to acquire a large block of shares, creating less supply. The basic economic reality kicks in at that point: more supply causes a decline in price, and less supply causes an increase in price. But now consider the underlying reality: The decision by an institutional investor (like a mutual fund) to buy or to sell a large number of shares of a company may have little or nothing to do with that company's fundamental strength or weakness. The decision may be a matter of portfolio balance, investment objective, or other reason that is not based on profit and loss or capitalization of the company.

A realistic combination of fundamental and technical analysis should be undertaken with the full realization that the two methods are not merely aspects of the same process. They are entirely separate and based on dissimilar assumptions. The fundamental approach relies on financial results and status; the technical approach is price-based.

The Dow Theory

Within the realm of technical indicators, a market premise tells you that price trends are reflected in longer-term movements, and that these are both predictable and recognizable. Whether this is entirely true or not is a matter of debate; but fundamental analysts may learn a great deal from studying the *Dow Theory* because it relates as much to fundamental analysis as it does to the technical side.

Dow Theory

a technical market theory based on the writings of Charles Dow. The theory is based on a belief that primary movements in stock indices establish and confirm marketwide trends.

The Dow Theory influences every investor's life on a daily basis. The well-known *Dow Jones Industrial Averages* (DJIA) is a collection of 30 stocks and a favorite method for judging the stock market. When the DJIA rises, it is a "good" day, and when it falls, it is a "bad" day. Eternally optimistic, the financial press selects positive words to describe up days—price surges, confidence, and so on—but more explanatory reasons for downward trends—that is, consolidation, profit-taking, and the like.

valuable resource
for more information about the DJIA, component stocks, weighting, and other links, check the Dow Jones website at http://averages.dowjones.com.

The DJIA is interesting to fundamental investors as a reflection of the Dow Theory, because the same principles underlying this theory can be applied on the fundamental side as well. Charles Dow was cofounder (along with partner Edward C. Jones) of the Dow Jones Corporation and of the publication that came to be known as the *Wall Street Journal.* During his lifetime, Dow published a series of essays in which he developed ideas for tracking corporate trends as well as stock prices. He believed in the principles of testing information by way of confirmation and breaking trends into three types: primary, secondary, and daily. While Dow himself did not solidify these theories into a distinct theory concerning the market, his ideas were applied after his death, and the Dow Theory came into being. First articulated by an associate of Dow's, Samuel Nelson, who published a book called *The ABCs of Stock Speculation,* the concept has since been further developed by Dow's successor as editor of the *Wall Street Journal*, Peter Hamilton.

Key Point

Although the Dow Theory is used today to track market price trends, its principles can also be effectively applied to fundamental analysis.

The Dow Theory as practiced today is a technical indicator; but it is valuable to tracking market trends over the long term, *and* can also be applied to the study of fundamental information. The concept of developing and tracking financial trends makes as much sense as it does for prices. Businesses depend on budgets and forecasts and unending financial analysis as part of monitoring profits. Business managers look for important indicators in order to take action quickly. For example, in an expense budget, if a month's expenses exceed the budget, management will want to know why. Steps need to be identified to stop a negative trend and bring expenses in line with the budget.

Market observers also look for pricing signals through the Dow Theory. A new trend is believed to be established when three specific

contrarian investing

a tendency among better-informed investors to anticipate coming trends and to trade accordingly— buying bargain-priced stocks when others are selling, and selling overpriced stocks when others continue to buy.

confirmation

the principle that a second indicator must move in the same direction as the primary indicator to establish a new trend; and that both indicators need to reverse direction before another change in trend is identified.

events take place. In a bull market, these events are the purchase of low-priced stocks when the market mood is negative; earnings growth in companies whose stock prices are low; and the discovery by the market as a whole of the value in stocks, which leads to greater demand. In a bear market, the three events are the sale of high-priced stocks by better-informed investors; a dwindling supply of willing buyers at current prices; and acceleration in the sale of shares, causing further price declines.

Most people recognize these generalized trend observations as *contrarian investing* standards, the tendency among better-informed investors to make decisions in directions opposite that of the broader market.

In addition to the three-part definition of contrarian tendencies among investors as a means for identifying a trend, the Dow Theory also requires *confirmation*. This is a process of checking one indicator against another. According to the Dow Theory, a new trend is established only if and when the Dow Jones Transportation Average follows the DJIA in moving away from its previous level; and the new trend stays in effect until both of these indices have reversed direction. In this sense, the transportation average confirms the DJIA.

The Dow Theory has become institutionalized as the major indicator of the market—even with equal news coverage given to the S&P 500 and the NASDAQ indices—that most people consider the point change in the DJIA as representing the entire market. However, as interesting as the indices are in tracking markets, the theories first put forth by Charles Dow have strong and specific applications in fundamental analysis.

Just as stock prices can be tracked, confirmed, and broken out into primary or secondary movements, so can financial data. The very nature of trend analysis and the use of ratios expressed as part of moving averages, forms an intelligent system for grasping the importance of financial trends over time—and for quantifying those trends as very significant or temporary in nature. Because most people follow more than one fundamental indicator (or use combinations of fundamental and technical data), confirmation is a natural process and it adds value. If one indicator implies a change in direction in earnings, for example, one way to verify the information is to check other indicators to see whether an expected shift is occurring there as well. Looking at indicators in isolation can be misleading; but when two or more different indicators tell you the same thing, that is very strong evidence.

The Random Walk Hypothesis

The market is not predictable, nor is it easily tracked with a few indicators. The purpose of analysis is to attempt to bring some order to chaos and actually improve the estimates you need to make. That is, the better and more reliable your information, the better your decisions. Even so, some people believe that if you watch prices as part of your program of analysis, you are wasting your time because price movement is entirely random.

The *random walk hypothesis* states that all price change in the short term is random. It is a kind of "chaos theory" because it relies on the idea that supply and demand exist in varying and often offsetting degrees so that no daily price movement can ever be the result of a clear or predictable cause.

> **random walk hypothesis**
> a theory concerning the stock market that all price movement is random because it results from a range of supply and demand causes.

Most analysts detest the random walk hypothesis. As long as someone is paid, by fee or commission, to tell you how to invest, they rely on the idea that their knowledge and insight is superior or, at least, that you believe it. The random walk hypothesis tells us that advice is useless because there is no way to predict price direction. Adding to the complexity is a natural desire among investors to desire predictability. Many investors continue paying for advice even when the brokerage track record is dismal, because they simply want to believe that they will get better information by paying for it. So investors also tend to discount the random walk hypothesis. It is troubling. It suggests that price cannot be predicted.

Key Point
So many insiders hate the random walk hypothesis because, if it is true, then investors do not need to pay for advice.

If you look back at companies whose stock has grown significantly in value over many decades, you soon realize that the feature these companies have in common is primarily fundamental in nature: strong sales and earnings, exceptional competitive position, growing dividend payments, excellence in management . . . in other words, very little in the way of *random* events. Here again, you run into the inconsistencies between pricing models—that is, the random walk hypothesis—and the fundamental and proven historical record. Some well-managed companies have undergone periods of price volatility or decline, but that has not meant that they were poor long-term investments. So a test of any pricing hypothesis should be undertaken in recognition of the fact that these price theories have nothing to do with financial strength or management of the companies.

The fact is that, as interesting a theory as the random walk hypothesis is, the historical record contradicts it. You see, repeatedly, that strongly capitalized, highly competitive, well-managed corporations grow; their stock increases in value; competition does not overtake those companies; and in the long term, there is nothing at all random about it. The excellence in product or service, management, and internal controls is what makes the real difference between good and bad investments.

A comparison between the Dow Theory and the random walk hypothesis is interesting because, in many ways, they are opposites. Both relate to the technical (price) side of analysis, but beyond that there are no similarities. The Dow Theory states that pricing trends are very predictable if you study investor behavior and watch indices. The random walk hypothesis tells you that it makes no difference because price movement is unpredictable and even arbitrary. Random walk analysis is offered as truth in academic circles, but it is not a real-world theory because it is easily disproved by the historical record, based on a comparison between fundamental indicators and real market value growth over time.

Closely related to the random walk hypothesis is the *efficient market theory*. It is contradictory in the sense that randomness and efficiency are hardly the same thing. Whereas the random walk hypothesis states that price change is unpredictable, the efficient market theory assumes that price change is based on the efficiency of the supply and demand

efficient market theory

a belief about the market, stating that the current price of stock reflects all known information at any given time; the concept that pricing of stocks is efficient because it is based on the collective knowledge of the market.

market. Its tenet states that all known information about a company is allowed for and reflected in the current price. If this were true, then the next change in price would be unpredictable (and currently, at least, random) because its direction would be based on information not yet known.

Just as the random walk is unlikely based on the historical record, the efficient market theory is equally dubious. It gives a tremendous benefit of the doubt to the market, which is wildly chaotic, involves conflicting interests and types of investors or traders, and overreacts to current news. So price is the sum of a series of movements, corrections, misunderstandings, exaggerations, and late reaction to old news—hardly an efficient reflection of currently known information.

Key Point

As reassuring as the idea is of an "efficient" market, anyone who has invested—especially those who have lost money on a "sure thing"—know that the short-term market is really quite chaotic and unpredictable.

You will recognize a similarity between the random walk hypothesis and the efficient market theory. Both are fancied as reliable theories in academic circles, where professors may have never placed *real* money into *real* stocks. Second, both assume that any form of analytical study designed to anticipate trends, is virtually useless. These fatalistic beliefs may capture your imagination for the moment, but if you look to the long-term record, you quickly realize that there are clear distinctions. Well-managed companies perform profitably in the market and reward investors; and poorly managed or undercapitalized companies perform poorly and lead to losses or stagnation. Theories aside, a sincere analysis of the technical market theories demonstrates that the fundamentals ultimately determine value.

Theories about Risk

On a practical level, investors should be more concerned with identifying the very real risks they face when they buy stocks. Fundamental analysis helps you to identify and compare risks so that you may avoid the

risk tolerance
the level of risk appropriate to each individual investor, based on income, assets, knowledge, and experience; the amount of market risk and other forms of risk a person is able and willing to tolerate.

common problem of investing, unintentionally, in stocks beyond your *risk tolerance* level.

The relationship between risk and opportunity is direct and unavoidable. It is impossible to achieve maximum reward without also increasing risk, a point too often overlooked by investors. Fundamental analysis focuses on a company's operating results and capital strength in an attempt to quantify risk in fiscal terms; however, it is easy to overlook this because of the ever-present stock price. So a mistaken pattern many investors follow involves these steps:

1. An initial series of basic fundamental tests are performed (a check of sales and profits, dividend rate, and working capital ratios, for example).

2. A short list of viable stocks meeting an investor's criteria is established.

3. Ultimately, a selection is made based on recent stock price movements, cost levels, or high–low positioning of the stock.

This three-step process begins on a fundamental premise, but then reverts to a technical decision point. This is an appropriate system as long as you are aware of how you make decisions. The problem arises when, after developing a fundamentally based selection process, the actual decision is made on technical information, specifically price. The fact that stocks have dollar values distorts this process and may result in your creating a portfolio with a risk profile higher than you intended. There is a tendency among investors to think of $20 stocks as "more affordable" than $40 stocks, for example. In reality, those price levels are meaningless.

One company may have 30 million shares outstanding, valued at $20 each, for total capitalization of $600 million. Another may have 15 million shares outstanding, valued at $40 each; this corporation also has $600 million in capital. So the stock price means nothing. If capitalization is the key decision point in stock selection, the stock price is misleading, and instead of considering it, you would have more accurate information reviewing total capital instead.

> ## Key Point
>
> People often perceive "risk" as being related to a stock's price or price range. In fact, the price of a stock by itself reveals nothing. You need to investigate further.

The problem of pricing and price distortion is often seen on television financial news as well, where the sound bite is important but in-depth and accurate information is easily lost in the process. For example, if a nightly news report tells you that two local stocks both rose in value, how do you hear the information? Here is an example:

Stock A   closed at $66, up 4 points

Stock B   closed at $22, up 2 points

Which of these stocks did better? If you look only at the point level, you would conclude that Stock A rose twice as much as Stock B. But this is an error. These daily changes can be looked at in two different ways. Stock A's price rose 6 percent, and Stock B's price rose 9 percent; in other words, Stock B performed far better than Stock A. Another way to look at this is on the basis of a similar investment level. If you had $6,600 to invest, you could buy 100 shares of Stock A, and you would have earned $400 in this market. Or you could buy 300 shares of Stock B for the same money, and you would have profited by $600 (300 shares multiplied by a 2-point rise).

The distortion in apparent valuation arises from the way financial news is reported. It may further distort your perception of risks. For example, some investors conclude that higher-priced stocks contain greater risk, if only because it takes more capital to buy 100 shares. In fact, though, if fundamental attributes are identical, there is no difference in risk between buying 100 shares of a $66 dollar stock, and buying 300 shares of a $22 stock. Those with less capital will find lower-priced stocks more convenient to purchase in 100-share lots. But that distinction is a feature of individual capital and affordability, and not a feature of risk.

Once you accept the premise that risk and opportunity are two aspects of the same market phenomenon, you can analyze risk in a realistic way. However, there are many different types of risk and each should be evaluated as part of the overall investment decision. These include four

market risk

the risk that an investment's market value will fall or that stocks are purchased at the wrong time, so that a temporary downward price movement results in a paper loss that may take time to recover.

liquidity risk

(investment funds) the risk that funds may not be readily available in particular markets, which have high liquidity risk, versus other markets in which funds can be converted to cash very quickly, which contain low liquidity risk; (markets) the risk that buyers and sellers may not be easily matched. For example, in a slow real estate market, there will be more sellers than buyers so properties may not sell for the currently asked price; in the stock market, specialists ensure an orderly market by completing orders even when buyers and sellers are not matched.

primary areas of interest to stock market investors. The first, *market risk,* is the best known. It relates to the basic idea that your investments may lose value. Stocks rise and fall, and if they fall after you buy them, you stand to lose money. In addition to careful selection of stocks, you can minimize market risk by placing orders with your brokerage firm to automatically generate sales when specific events occur, such as a loss of a specified percentage of value.

The second is *liquidity risk*, which refers to how available your investment funds are to you. When you buy a house, it would require considerable time and expense to sell and remove your equity, or to refinance. So real estate is illiquid. When you invest in stocks, you can sell immediately for relatively small costs, and your money can be in your hands within a few days. So stocks are highly liquid.

A second definition of liquidity refers to the overall market itself. The availability of sellers to match buyers (and vice versa) is also called liquidity. In the stock market, the on-going auction of shares matches buyers and sellers continuously and the market is set up so that even when sellers are not readily available, a *specialist* will complete a transaction to maintain an orderly market.

A third risk is *lost opportunity risk*, the risk that every investor faces whenever limited capital is committed to a particular investment. This risk arises in numerous situations. For example, if your portfolio consists of stocks that have lost value or are remaining in a narrow trading range when the market as a whole is rising, having capital committed to those stock presents a lost opportunity. Another situation involves tying up stock to cover a short option position. If that option is exercised, the covered call writer has lost the opportunity to gain profits in the stock.

The fourth type of risk is *diversification risk*, the exposure created when too much capital is placed in a single stock or series of stocks. Effective diversification requires more than spreading money around in different stocks. If all of the stocks are similar in nature, subject to the same cyclical or economic forces, or likely to rise and fall in the same patterns, the portfolio is not effectively diversified. The risk is mitigated when capital is allocated among different market sectors such as energy, pharmaceuticals, and retail; different types of investments such as stocks, real estate, and savings); and different venues such as stocks and mutual funds as a collective stock market segment of your portfolio rather than different stocks.

Markets Matched to Risk Tolerance

Fundamental investors will tend to structure their portfolios not only based on financial attributes, but also in a way to mitigate all four of these risks. This requires a broad view of how capital is placed and left on deposit; how risks can be managed collectively; and how funds should be repositioned as circumstances change. The goal is not to completely eliminate risk, which is impossible, but to reduce all four types to a level that is acceptable.

specialist
an individual working in a stock exchange whose function is to ensure an orderly market, completing orders even when buyers and sellers are not equal.

lost opportunity risk
the risk that, due to the way investment capital is committed, other profit opportunities will be lost. The most common example involves buying stocks that remain at a set price, while other stocks rise in value.

diversification risk
the risk that a portfolio will not be invested in enough different issues, markets, or venues to ensure safety; a nondiversified portfolio is subject to the same cyclical or economic forces, which places the entire portfolio at greater risk.

Key Point

It is often suggested that you can eliminate risk but still outperform the market. That is contradictory, and impossible. The goal should not be to eliminate risk, but to reduce it to a manageable level.

Investors who devote a large portion of their total investment capital to the stock market will recognize the four types of risk and act accordingly. It would be a mistake to invest your entire portfolio in one market or in one sector or stock. The market risk would be unacceptable for most people; lost opportunity risk would be high; and diversification risk would be very high. Only liquidity risk would be eliminated with a reckless program involving a singular investment strategy.

One effective way to diversify within the stock market is through the use of both individually owned stocks and mutual funds. Using balanced funds or bonds funds further diversifies a market portfolio between stocks (equity positions) and bonds (debt positions). While mutual funds are relatively liquid, *exchange traded funds* (ETFs) are types of mutual funds whose shares trade just like stocks over exchanges. So diversification and liquidity can be achieved together via the ETF market. This solves many of the risk-specific problems stock market investors face, by reducing market, liquidity, and diversification risk in a single market venue.

Individuals may also want to keep a portion of their portfolio is savings, certificates of deposit, and other highly liquid money market accounts, to ensure that a portion of the total investment portfolio is available immediately. In addition, proponents of *asset allocation* are quick to point out that investors should also keep some of their money invested in real estate. While down payments and mortgages may be huge drains on investors, it is not necessary to set aside a large portion of capital in real estate, for two reasons. First, if you own your own home you already have an investment position in real estate. Second, you do not have to own properties directly to allocate your portfolio among stocks, bonds, and real estate. You can invest in real estate in many other ways. For example, buying shares in mortgage pools places you in a debt position in secured first mortgages. You can also buy shares of exchange traded funds that invest only in real estate stocks. Finally, you can also buy

exchange traded funds

types of mutual funds with a pre-identified basket of stocks in its portfolio and whose shares trade over public exchanges just like individual stocks.

asset allocation

a strategic portfolio management technique for identifying how capital should be divided among major markets (usually stocks, bonds, and real estate), based on current market and economic conditions, risk tolerance, and individual investment goals.

units in limited partnerships and similar highly specialized investments. So there are many venues for buying real estate beyond directly owner-ship of investment properties.

In any and all of these portfolio management concerns, fundamental analysis applies. It is not only a stock-related function, although it is most closely associated with stocks. This is true because so many of the fundamental tests are derived from financial statements. However, in all types of investments, fundamental analysis should include tests of investment viability. This is especially true in considering another form of risk that has two parts: inflation and taxes.

Key Point

The combination of inflation and taxes is one of the biggest inhibitors to market profits. The more taxes you pay, and the higher inflation, the more you need just to break even. And the more you need, the higher the risk you need to take.

The *inflation risk* relates to the risk that inflation—the loss of purchasing power of money—will offset some or all of the profits you gain from investments. If you seek highly safe investments, you may end up placing money in accounts whose yield is lower than current inflation. In this situation, you lose money and suffer inflation risk. The *tax risk* is similar in the sense that you need to consider the net gains from investing after paying both federal and state taxes. These risks become especially important when considered together.

One effective method for fundamental analysis of investments—as a starting point—is to look at inflation and taxes together, and calculate what rate of return you will need to break even. This *breakeven calculation* is essential, especially when your tax liability is high, because it is possible that investments will be so conservative that, on an after-inflation and after-tax basis, you may lose even when the simple return appears positive.

inflation risk
the risk that investment net yield will be lower than inflation. Consequently, your portfolio loses value when purchasing power (after-inflation value) is taken in to account.

tax risk
the exposure of investments to tax liabilities. Investment yield and risk should be evaluated on an after-tax basis to allow for the tax risk in the equation.

breakeven calculation

a formula used to determine the required breakeven point for investments, considering the effects of both inflation and income taxes. To calculate, divide the current inflation rate by the rate of after-tax income. (After-tax income is 100 minus an individual's tax rate, including both federal and state.)

To calculate breakeven, you need to know two factors. First is the current rate of inflation. This can be found at the website of the U.S. Census Bureau (http://www.census.gov). Second is your effective tax rate. This is the rate of tax you pay on your taxable income. Be sure to consider both federal and state rates. The breakeven formula is:

$$\frac{I}{100 - T} = B$$

where

I = inflation rate

T = effective tax rate

B = breakeven rate

For example, if you assume a 3 percent rate of inflation, and you pay 15 percent federal plus 6 percent in state tax (combined 21 percent), your breakeven is 3.8 percent:

$$\frac{3}{100 - 21} = 3.8\%$$

Table 2.1 summarizes breakeven rates required for various tax brackets (combined federal and state) and rates of inflation.

In examining this table, you can see that the greater your tax liability, and the higher the rate of inflation, the more you need to earn from your overall investments, just to break even. This type of analysis is fundamental because it involves a practical evaluation of profitability. When viewed comparatively among investments, and with risk levels in mind, breakeven analysis is a critical step to take. For example, in looking at two or more stocks, it is tempting to pick the one with the greatest potential for short-term price increases. But that also means exposing yourself to price volatility, a technical risk. This means that just as prices may rise, they may also fall, an example of how opportunity and risk are inescapably related.

TABLE 2.1 Breakeven Rates for Tax Brackets (in percent)

INFLATION RATE

Tax Rate	1%	2%	3%	4%	5%	6%
10%	1.1%	2.2%	3.3%	4.4%	5.6%	6.7%
12	1.1	2.3	3.4	4.5	5.7	6.8
14	1.2	2.3	3.5	4.7	5.8	7.0
16	1.2	2.4	3.6	4.8	6.0	7.1
18	1.2	2.4	3.7	4.9	6.1	7.3
20%	1.3%	2.5%	3.8%	5.0%	6.3%	7.5%
22	1.3	2.6	3.8	5.1	6.4	7.7
24	1.3	2.6	3.9	5.3	6.6	7.9
26	1.4	2.7	4.1	5.4	6.8	8.1
28	1.4	2.8	4.2	5.6	6.9	8.3
30%	1.4%	2.9%	4.3%	5.7%	7.1%	8.6%
32	1.5	2.9	4.4	5.9	7.4	8.8
34	1.5	3.0	4.5	6.1	7.6	9.1
36	1.6	3.1	4.7	6.3	7.8	9.4
38	1.6	3.2	4.8	6.5	8.1	9.7
40%	1.7%	3.3%	5.0%	6.7%	8.3%	10.0%
42	1.7	3.4	5.2	6.9	8.6	10.3
44	1.8	3.6	5.4	7.1	8.9	10.7
46	1.9	3.7	5.6	7.4	9.3	11.1
48	1.9	3.8	5.8	7.7	9.6	11.5

In the next chapter, you will see how the basic information you find about companies—the audited financial statement—is put together and presented. This chapter also explains why you cannot depend solely on the audited statement and why you need to look beyond to ensure that the information you use in decision making is accurate and reliable.

The Audited Statement—Flawed but Useful

It is a very sad thing that nowadays there is so little useless information.
—Oscar Wilde, in *Saturday Review*, 1894

Investors have traditionally depended on the rock-solid reputation of auditing firms. These independent firms were—and the ones still with us are—charged with critically reviewing the books and records of their client corporations and rendering opinions about the reliability of those records. That changed, however, due to Enron and their auditing firm, Arthur Andersen.

Until the discovery of Arthur Andersen's Enron problem, the reputation of the auditing industry was virtually unquestioned. Even though a string of lawsuits and reversed opinions should have signaled problems, they did not. Even the passage of new laws had not changed the way accounting firms did their business. Other accounting firms had their share of problems, too, including:

- Deloitte & Touche, which did not notify Adelphia's auditing committee about irregularities by the Rigas family
- KPMG, which was criticized for its handling of Xerox Corporation's audit in an SEC investigation (and leading to a five-year restatement of $6.4 billion in revenues)

- PricewaterhouseCoopers, which was criticized and investigated for not red-flagging Tyco unauthorized executive compensation

All of these well-publicized cases demonstrate that there was enough blame to go around among the major accounting firms in addition to Arthur Andersen.

A basic trust issue has arisen and it has ramifications for investors. In the case of Arthur Andersen, no central controls were initiated to prevent abuse; on the contrary, the rule at the firm was to increase revenues on a decentralized basis. One business magazine described the auditing firm's internal structure as "a loose confederation of fiefdoms covering different geographic markets . . . unable to respond swiftly to crises or even to govern itself decisively."[1]

You can depend on audited financial statements, but not as completely as in the past. In this chapter, you will find out how audited statements are compiled and why you need to look beyond those statements to ensure that you have reliable information.

How Audits Are *Really* Conducted

In the audited statement process, an independent auditing firm is expected to conduct a review of the transactions and accounting policies of a corporation; examine internal controls; make recommendations for improvements in procedures; and issue an opinion letter. If the auditor's opinion is that the books and records are accurate and reliable, the opinion letter states as much. If for any reason the auditor believes the books and records are not reliable, that opinion is stated in the letter. The purpose of this exercise is to ensure everyone—stockholders, analysts, and regulators—that the books are being kept properly and according to the rules.

Key Point
The audit is supposed to be independent, aimed at advising stockholders about the accuracy of financial statements. In practice, you cannot rely on audited statements to objectively point out flaws in corporate financial reporting.

The system is full of problems, however. You cannot rely completely on the audit process nor on the objectivity of the auditing firm. The problem begins with the fact that corporations pay auditing firms to prepare their books. It is made worse by the fact that a substantial portion of the auditing company's revenue is derived from nonaudit work that it performs for the same client. So the incentive is to keep clients happy, and that means it can become a problem if and when disagreements arise over accounting decisions and the way that transactions are reported.

This was precisely what occurred when Arthur Andersen was auditing the books of Enron. There were numerous questionable practices and deceptions in the accounting system, including inaccurate operating results. Enron's books were complex and misleading. Arthur Andersen's Houston office knew of this problem but did not blow the whistle. Why? Enron was a huge client of the company and represented a good source of revenues. The home office of Arthur Andersen had instituted its own procedures requiring senior partners to generate nonauditing revenue that was equal to or higher than audit revenues. So the senior auditors were under pressure to keep clients and to increase revenues, which is not a healthy environment for auditors who are supposed to maintain independence and objectivity.

The problems were not unique to Arthur Andersen. Most of the large auditing firms had settled lawsuits from shareholders over many years, admitted inaccuracies in their statements, and had lived with their own conflicts of interest. The situation has not changed today. Rather than considered the corporate scandals as a sign that the industry needed to fix its conflict problems, the accounting industry has treated the problem as a public relations matter.

A lot of lip service has been paid to compliance with new laws and regulations, but the industry has only found ways to get around the legal attempts to do away with its conflict of interest. What this means for investors is that more caution is required. The fact is that the majority of audited statements are accurate and fair. It is not safe to rely completely on what those statements reveal, however, for several reasons:

1. The accounting rules are so complex that it is possible to create a number of different outcomes and to find justification within the rules.

2. The auditing rules are slow to change because the structure of the industry and its own regulatory system are complex.

3. Even with new laws designed to eliminate auditing firm conflicts of interest, it is too easy for firms to get around the rules. To this day, auditing firms continue performing both audit and nonaudit work for the same clients.

4. Even with the most reliable financial statements, you need to perform your own fundamental tests. Even with a movement under way to improve corporate transparency, little chance has been seen in the way that corporations report to shareholders. If you are not able or willing to go beyond the statements to perform added research, you should be working with a financial planner or advisor who does know how to perform those tests. (Chapter 4 provides guidelines for navigating corporate websites and finding additional information.)

Key Point

The concept of corporate transparency states that investors should be able to see what is really taking place. In practice, current reporting standards are anything but transparent—even after the reported scandals from a few years ago.

Investors need to supplement the audited statement with fundamental tests of their own. It is not rational to trust audited statements as in the past, because recent history has demonstrated that the firms conducting audits do not always act objectively or independently.

generally accepted accounting principles (GAAP)

a series of rules, opinions, and guidelines governing accounting and auditing practices and used within the industry to regulate the decisions and activities of independent auditors.

How GAAP Works

The accounting system in use today, also called *generally accepted accounting principles (GAAP)*, is not a single set of rules or procedures; it is the combination of many opinions, reports, studies, and publications put out by several different sources.

The GAAP system doesn't reside in any one place. It has many parts and organizations. First is the Financial Accounting Standards Board (FASB), an organization founded in 1973 (http://www.fasb.org). This organization has the final say on how audits are conducted, how financial information is interpreted, and how reports are prepared. Both the Securities and Exchange Commission (SEC) (http://www.sec.gov) and the industry association, the American Institute of Certified Public Accountants (AICPA) (http://www.aicpa.org) recognize the authority of the FASB.

The FASB itself provides a very clear definition of the importance of consistency in accounting standards:

> Accounting standards are essential to the efficient functioning of the economy because decisions about the allocation of resources rely heavily on credible, concise, transparent and understandable financial information.[2]

In spite of this standard, in practice auditors continue to have a motivation to respond to their clients (who, after all, pay the bills) rather than to follow a truly independent and objective set of auditing guidelines. Additionally, the FASB does not make the task of following standards easy. It has published thousands of pages of guidelines, which are technical, complex and at times contradictory. One former corporate CEO, Walter Wriston of Citigroup, pointed to the existence of more than 800 pages of FASB guidelines on the single topic of derivatives, for example.

Key Point

Accounting standards are so complex that the average person could never sort them out. Even accountants are challenged by the sheer complexity of their own system.

The complexities of published GAAP guidelines are not limited to FASB. The industry association, AICPA also issues opinions and guidelines for its members. Collectively, GAAP consists of the two major organizations FASB and AICPA; as well as federal and state regulatory agencies, various subcommittees and rulemaking groups, and published books and magazine articles on accounting, auditing, legal, and regulatory matters. So GAAP is a culture rather than a single, definitive body of rules ands regulations. Unfortunately for investors, this also means that within the high volume of complex and technical opinions, it is easy to find justification for just about any position short of outright fraud. The accounting industry is complex to begin with; for the nonaccountant, the GAAP standards are too broad and too technical to be of much use.

The problem today is not only that GAAP is so complex, but also that accounting firms—having been sued endlessly by deceived stockholders and regulators—now design their auditing disclosures not so much to provide information and transparency, but to protect themselves from future lawsuits. Former SEC Chairman Harvey Pitt explained:

> Today, disclosures are made not to inform, but to avoid liability . . . We cannot afford a system, like the present one, that facilitates failure rather than success. Accounting firms have important public responsibilities. We have had far too many financial and accounting failures . . . we must put a stop to a vicious cycle that has been in evidence for far too many years."[3]

Pitt was accurate in his description. However, even with changes in the law concerning how audits are conducted, there has been little improvement in the problem since his statements. Investors cannot reply exclusively on audited financial statements, but need to look beyond the columns of numbers, to the disclosures in the notes to the financial statements.

Disclosures in the Footnotes

The problems of the accounting industry are complex and far-reaching. For you, it means that the long-trusted audited financial statement cannot be accepted at face value as it has been in the past. Everyone has to adopt the philosophy that even independently audited financial statements have to be verified and their information subjected to your own ratios and tests. This task is not difficult. You can find corporate disclosures in the annual and quarterly statement footnotes for any listed company. Most of these are available online.

Valuable Resource

To find free annual reports online, check these websites:
  Annual Report Service at http://www.annualreportservice.com
  Public Register's Annual Report Service at http://www.prars.com
  Report Gallery at http://www.reportgallery.com

Most people refer to the footnotes included as part of the annual statement to supplement information shown on the summarized financial statements. These notes can run to over 100 pages in many cases, so they are daunting—the good news is you do not need to read all of them. Many are technical and deal with accounting issues, foreign exchange, valuation, and disclosures of little interest to anyone other than accountants. Some footnotes and supplementary schedules, however, are very interesting. The kinds of things most people look for in the footnotes include:

1. Details of operating results by division, unit, or subsidiary.

2. Multiyear summaries of key results (sometimes 10 years or more).

3. Information about the nature of changes other than dollars and cents. (For retail corporations, as one example, you can compare numbers of outlets, retail square footage from year to year, and similar revealing statistics.)

4. Unusual items this year that are not typical. "Nonrecurring" or "extraordinary" items affect results but should be removed from any trend analysis. They include events like the sale of a major operating unit (this affects current year income but also changes long-term trend analysis company-wide because a sold subsidiary is no longer part of the mix); capital gains and losses (e.g., if a company sells a building or land, it will report a large amount of income, but it is not part of the year-to-year results); and accounting adjustments (e.g., if a company changes its method for valuation of inventory, it has a big impact on total profits).

Key Point

The process of tracking a company's growth is complicated if each year's financial statements include an array of complicated nonrecurring or extraordinary items.

There may be many types of adjustments and changes in the footnotes, and everything is supposed to be disclosed there. Many corporations operate a complex series of operating units other than the business for which they are best known; even then a study of operating results in detail may reveal important information. Altria Corporation, for example, known for its primary business, Philip Morris cigarette sales, is not just a tobacco company. If you check this company's homepage (http://www.altria.com), you will discover that the company operates four major divisions. Philip Morris domestic and international sales are the two largest; but the company also owns Kraft Foods, which is one of the largest food corporations in the world with dozens of brand names. Altria also operates Philip Morris Capital Corporation, a leasing company. A study of the year-to-year trends within the Altria umbrella reveals that some units are moving upward in sales and profits, while others (like domestic tobacco) are declining from year to year. So looking at the consolidated mix of business is revealing only on a corporate-wide scale. The real trends are found in the details, and that requires more study.

Key Point
The most interesting operating trends for corporations are often found not in the consolidated statements, but in a study of major operating units.

The footnotes provide a wealth of data and they are worth checking. The next chapter shows by example how to get onto corporate websites and check for a specific list of items not found on the financial statements. If you are uncomfortable delving into the footnotes, then at the very least, you should be working with a professional advisor who can perform that service for you.

Your list of additional information should be quite limited. One mistake people have made is falling into the belief that fundamental analysis requires an in-depth analysis and study of the entire financial statement. You will be most effective if you identify a few important trends and follow them over time, to ensure that you are able to track financial performance or strength of a company. That is the real purpose to the analytical process.

The Sarbanes-Oxley Act and Auditing Safeguards

The problem of reporting results accurately is substantial. Managers interested in giving stockholders all that they need face a series of legal hurdles as well as accounting complexities. In 2002, the *Sarbanes-Oxley Act*

(SOX) was passed by Congress to establish standards for auditors as well as for corporations in how conflicts of interest are to be eliminated, and in how corporations must disclose financial results to stockholders and to regulators.

Under the new law, SOX, major changes were made in the following areas:

1. *Public Company Accounting Oversight Board.* SOX sets up a special board to regulate auditors. In the past, the accounting industry was self-regulating; but history has shown that this was not effective. Now the SEC has the authority, through this board, to perform four specific functions: (1) set standards for audits, (2) inspect accounting firm procedures and records, (3) investigate violations, and (4) impose sanctions when needed.

Sarbanes-Oxley Act (SOX)
a 2002 federal law regulating accountants, executives, and securities analysts in reporting to the public and in disclosing potential conflicts of interest; and established to increase regulatory funding to investigate corporate practices by the Securities and Exchange Commission (SEC).

Key Point

The provision under SOX to impose outside regulation on the accounting industry is incredible. The complete failure of the industry to regulate itself, alone, points out how little investors can trust in the independence of the audit.

2. *Auditor independence.* Most big accounting firms have historically performed a broad range of nonaudit services for their audit clients. This has led to two types of conflict of interest. First, auditors are less likely to challenges improper activities of clients when large nonaudit fees are involved, out of fear of losing the client. Second, it is likely that auditors end up reviewing their own work when, for example, the same firm has designed and installed internal audit systems. Under SOX, many specific nonaudit services are prohibited if and when the firms also perform audits for the same clients. Under the same provision, a firm may not perform an audit if any senior management of the firm worked for the accounting firm within the past year.

3. *Corporate responsibility.* Publicly listed companies are required to appoint audit committees, which are responsible for hiring and paying an auditing firm; overseeing the auditors; receiving and reviewing reports; and resolving disputes that arise from audits. Senior managers cannot interact directly with auditors.

   A related provision under this section makes chief executive officers (CEOs) and chief financial officers (CFOs) personally responsible for certifying that financial statements are complete and accurate. Both civil and criminal penalties can be imposed for false certification. The same CEOs and CFOs are forbidden from attempting to influence the outcome of audits. The penalties for infractions of the SOX rules could include monetary fines, prison terms, and permanent bar from serving as officers or directors of any public companies.

4. *Financial disclosure rules.* The law requires companies to explain all important adjustments proposed by auditors, even when those suggestions did not end up changing the financial statements. (The requirement extends to transactions off the balance sheet as well as those included.) An *off-balance sheet transaction* can include an important obligation or entity that can affect future profit reporting.

off-balance sheet transaction
any transaction of a company not shown on the balance sheet or operating statement. These include lease obligations, contingent liabilities, and unconsolidated subsidiary company operating results.

5. *Analyst conflict of interest.* SOX requires that securities analysts follow specific rules and make disclosures to clients. At least four types of conflict of interest have been chronic in the Wall Street establishment in the past, including:

   a. Compensation is often based in part on how well an analyst participates in underlying a company's stock.

   b. The analyst's firm may be compensated in part from companies on which research reports are published.

   c. The investing banking personnel within the firm may influence analysts to issue favorable reports on companies whose stock is underwritten by the company.

   d. In the past, analysts issuing negative reports suffered retaliation, further pressuring those analysts to report favorably on companies when investing banking relationships were in effect.

Under SOX analysts are required to disclose any interests in a company's stock; and companies are required to separate operating units between investment banking and research activities. The new rules clarify, for example, that if an analyst's firm is underwriting a stock, then the analyst cannot also recommend the stock to his or her clients.

6. *Regulatory funding.* SOX authorized $776 million in additional budget for the SEC to carry out oversight and enforcement duties under the Act. Throughout the 1990s, the SEC budget remained at the same level even though its obligations grew. The increased budget helped the SEC to catch up to its basic staffing and audit requirements, as well as to meet its new duties. These included salary increases for existing regulatory staff; improved technological systems; and hiring of at least 200 additional investigators and staff.

The Corporate Scandals

How serious were the corporate scandals that came to light in 2001 and 2002? Many individuals lost all or most of their investment savings as a consequence of the scandals, in which several corporations defrauded stockholders. This occurred through artificial earnings reports, exaggerated revenues, and off-balance sheet transactions. Today, many people who lost money have simply left the stock market and will not return.

Key Point

The corporate scandals did not just shake up the accounting industry or highlight abuses by some greedy corporate executives. Thousands of investors lost their life savings and have been permanently damaged by the abuses.

The scandals were well publicized and involved some big-name companies. However, there were many more obscure investigations affecting all of the big accounting firms to some degree, and all of the major Wall Street securities firms.

In 2002 the state of New York settled with Merrill Lynch over numerous claims charging conflict of interest. Merrill paid $100 million in fines, but beyond that one incident, Merrill Lynch is estimated to have paid out over $2 billion in penalties for its abuses and conflicts of interest.[4] The problems were, indeed, widespread. In early 2003 New York, along with the National Association of Securities Dealers (NASD) and the SEC, assessed $1.4 billion in fines against ten of the largest Wall Street firms.

The new law and even the huge fines did not change the way the Wall Street firms operate. Individual investors cannot trust established firms to provide them with objective advice, because the corporate culture of Wall Street wants everyone to buy and no one to sell. By mid-2002, after the major corporate scandals hit the papers, and after widespread news about analysts' internal conflicts of interest, the big firms continued to favor buy over sell recommendations. On July 1, only 5.8 percent of Merrill Lynch recommendations were to sell; 3.5 percent at Prudential; 1.5 percent at Goldman Sachs; 1.0 percent at Lehman; 0.9 percent at JPMorgan Chase; and 0.4 percent at Credit Suisse First Boston. Among the big brokerage firms, only Morgan Stanley broke out above the 3 percent and below range for sell recommendations, with 20.9 percent of their total advice to clients to sell.[5]

Key Point

The record comparing buy and sell recommendations by big Wall Street firms highlights the intrinsic nature of the problem. Nothing has changed.

The point to remember here is that in the aftermath of big headlines about corporate scandals, the complicity of accounting firms, and the outright lack of good advice among the largest Wall Street analysts, the situation has not really changed. It is the same as it has been since stock markets were first devised hundred of years ago: No one whose compensation is based on making a high volume of buy recommendations is going to give clients objective advice. This is why you need to be able to perform your own fundamental analysis, even if only limited to a few very basic tests of profitability and capital strength. Those tests alone are worth far more than the unreliable and inherently self-serving advice investors get from security analysts.

The scandals pointed out serious flaws and abuses in both publicly listed corporations and accounting forms. But these events also serve as an ongoing reminder to every investor that it does not make sense to put trust in securities analysts or in the audited statements published by companies. The scandals bring up several points everyone needs to remember, and the following suggestions make sense:

1. *Diversify your portfolio.* Many people lost money because they invested in the wrong companies; they trusted the Wall Street experts and relied on audited financial statements. For a while, Enron was the new favorite stock on Wall Street and thousands of people put their money (and their trust) in Enron stock. Even the esteemed Dow Jones Corporation was duped, and placed Enron on the Dow Jones Utilities Averages, which subsequently rose impressively (based, of course, on Enron's artificial earnings). Even though the numbers were false, it remains good advice to diversify. It makes no sense to put more money into a single stock than you can afford to lose, given worst-case planning.

2. *Develop a sensible but simplified plan to check the numbers yourself.* You simply cannot rely exclusively on audited financial statements. This dose of reality is painful to accept for everyone, but it is reality nonetheless. You need to develop a short list of simple but important fundamental tests, and use those tests to examine the numbers for yourself.

3. *Never trust someone else to take care of your capital with the same care you exercise.* The age-old lesson concerning money is that no one else is going to be as careful as you are. The painful aspect of this is that greed motivates people. Many corporate executives pirated millions of dollars away from stockholders in the form of bonus compensation and stock options, and they showed a complete lack of concern for investors, employees, or customers. Those corporate executives were responsible to stockholders and were trusted to do all they could to make their investments safe and profitable. The vast majority of executives perform ethically, but a small number betrayed everyone and enriched themselves. This points out, once again, the need to diversify, verify, and never trust anyone exclusively.

Why Audited Statements Do Not Tell the Whole Story

While you cannot rely exclusively on the audited financial statement, this does not mean that statements are useless. In fact, they are valuable in what they do reveal. The starting point for trend analysis should be found on financial statements, but along with that you also need to be able to spot emerging problems or questionable reported numbers. For example, if a company is reporting declining sales, increasing expenses, and ever-higher net losses, everyone will agree that the trend is negative. But what if, at the same time, the company's *working capital* remains strong and consistent from one year to the next? The numbers simply don't add up and something is wrong when this occurs.

working capital
the funds available to a corporation to fund ongoing operations for the immediate future, and a test applied to test and compare cash flow. Working capital is the net difference between current assets and current liabilities.

Working capital is considered one of the most important financial aspects of corporate strength, a quick view of the company's effectiveness is managing cash flow. When a series of net losses occurs, you would expect to see working capital weaken. However, there is a way that corporations can bolster working capital to create the appearance that it is managing cash flow effectively, even when it loses money every year. By issuing new bonds or acquiring new long-term loans, companies can keep their cash balances up, thus keeping working capital at high levels. The problem with this practice is that it artificially creates a good ratio, deceiving those fundamental analysts who look only at the cash flow question.

The solution: In evaluating working capital, you also need to track total capitalization and to monitor the company's long-term debt (bonds and notes). If you discover that a corporation is creating effective working capital by increasing long-term debt, it is usually a highly negative sign for several reasons. First, the practice creates an artificially positive-looking outcome but it is deceptive. Second, as long-term debt is increased, it places an ever-increasing burden on future cash flow and robs stockholders of future dividends. Because the corporation will have to repay the long-term debt *and* make interest payments, the higher that debt and the less profits there are to continue funding working capital or to declare dividends.

All financial tests can be confirmed (or contradicted) by looking at related ratios. In this example, a comparison between operating results (with net losses reported) and working capital did not make sense. When the analysis went to an additional step, it became clear what the company was doing to create the illusion of cash flow strength, and the real story became clear. This is an example of how fundamental analysis can and should be performed.

Although the examination of financial ratios is more technical than some people want to do, these tests are not difficult to perform. In the next chapter you will see just how easily you can navigate through an online annual statement and find answers for yourself. The point to be emphasized here is that you cannot rely on audited financial statements for answers. In the case of the deceptively created working capital scenario, it is doubtful that an auditor would include an honest explanation in the footnotes to the financial statements. Perhaps they *should*, but that level of transparency has not yet been created among U.S.-listed companies. Auditing firms working for those companies do *not* protect investors by disclosing the kinds of problems that you should be concerned about. The audited statement is one of many tools that you can use to begin your own examination of a corporation's profitability and capital strength. But it is a mistake to assume that the independent audit is actually independent. The auditing firm works for the corporation and not for the stockholder. That is an unpleasant fact of life, but even with the Sarbanes-Oxley Act in effect, investors and stockholders remain on their own when it comes to protecting their interests.

Core Earnings Adjustments

One final observation concerning audited financial statements: The reported outcomes are based on the GAAP system, which means that the conclusions are far from accurate. You need to take steps to adjust reported results to identify likely future trends.

The results you see on an audited statement include everything, even profits from nonrecurring events. So if a company sells a major operating unit or has capital gains, those profits are included in the "bottom line" even though they won't occur again next year. The GAAP system enables this to occur, so the reported earnings are distorted. It is the equivalent of a consumer going to the bank and requesting a loan, and including in "annual income" a $200,000 profit from selling a home a few months before. The banker would adjust the numbers and tell that person that the home sale cannot be included in "annual income." That is precisely what corporations do in their financial statements—and it is acceptable under the GAAP system.

Key Point

Corporate reporting is self-serving and exceptional, and the rules allow distortions of reported profits. These practices deceive investors, so everyone needs to look beyond the official and auditor-approved statement to find the truth. One thing GAAP does not reveal in every instance is what is really going on.

---

core earnings

the revenues and profits a corporation earns during the year from its primary business activity, and excluding nonrecurring revenues.

The reported profit and loss each year should be adjusted to remove all noncore earnings of the corporation. The *core earnings* that remain should be only those sources of revenue generated from the corporation's primary (core) business.

The concept of core earnings was originated by Standard & Poor's Corporation, and is used to rate corporate bonds. However, it makes equal sense to adjust core earnings when comparing two or more corporate financial statements. For example, if you are comparing two different corporate financial statements, are they actually comparable? One may have substantial noncore revenues, while the other has none. So the GAAP-based operating statements will not be reliable or even comparable. Core earnings adjustments can be varied and complex, but the likely major adjustments usually involve a small number of items: capital gains or losses, profits from the sale of a subsidiary or operating unit, and one-time accounting or valuation changes, for example.

One reason that there is widespread resistance among accountants and corporations to a realistic level of transparency is that it would reveal some unpleasant truths. Reporting core earnings leads to another issue: the reporting of core net worth, which is the company's real net worth including *all* liabilities. Today, corporations often do not list their pension liabilities, for example. If they did, many corporations would have no net worth and even a large negative net worth. This is a very troubling idea, but it is not just a theory, it is reality. And before any investors decide to buy stock in a corporation, they should know, at the very least, whether that company is worth anything.

In June 2005 it was reported that General Motors, which has the nation's largest pension fund, has inflated its net worth by $38 billion due to unlisted pension liabilities. If GM were to list this liability, it would have negative net worth. (GM's most recently reported shareholders' equity was $27.7 billion, so an adjustment downward of $38 billion would result in *negative* net worth of over $10 billion.) Similar adjustments would move IBM's equity from $30 billion down to $8 billion, and Ford Motor's from $16 down to $4.7 billion.[6]

The problem is not just that liabilities are not reported on companies' balance sheets. These practices are acceptable and legal under GAAP. It is unlikely that the system will be changed any time soon as long as some of the country's largest corporations might be shown to have no value whatsoever—or even a *negative* net worth. The very fact that GAAP allows corporations to omit important liabilities points to major flaws in the system.

Key Point

If corporations were required to report everything, it would come to light that many of the country's largest companies—like General Motors—are worthless and have no net worth. An even bigger problem is that under the GAAP system, leaving out major liabilities is allowed. Investors do *not* get an accurate picture of profits or even of the value of stock.

Anyone can examine the financial statement footnotes to find major core earnings or core net worth adjustments and to recalculate reported profits and losses to make comparisons between companies more accurate.

It is unfortunate that the accounting industry has not stepped forward and made adjustments to its reporting standards to perform this obvious function for investors. Eventually, GAAP may be reformed so that core earnings adjustments can be made. In the meantime, U.S.-based corporations continue to underestimate the importance of transparency, and may fall behind in the new global market that is emerging today.

For example, in the rapidly-growing market in China, an especially complex business environment includes publicly listed companies that may report its operating results on a number of different standards, including U.S.-style GAAP, *international accounting standards* (IAS), and Hong Kong GAAP. Because the three systems would create potentially different outcomes, many publicly listed companies report their results showing all three. This concept is sensible and it should be a logical form of corporate transparency, enabling anyone to compare corporate financial statements without needing to delve into the complexities of financial statement footnotes. The same philosophy would make perfect sense in the United States.

Investors and analysts would be able to make complete sense out of audited statements of U.S. companies if the spirit of transparency were taken to its logical and reasonable end. Financial statements should be issued showing three different outcomes:

- *GAAP.* This is the version you get today, the interpretation of corporate valuation of assets and liabilities allowed by the rules, and summaries of sales, costs, expenses, and profits that may include noncore sources of revenue.

- *Statutory.* This version would be the same as what gets reported to the government for tax purposes. Corporations rarely publish their tax returns for investors to see; but it would be revealing in comparison, because many adjustments are possible. A comparison between the GAAP-based report and the tax-based report would be enlightening to investors. Even though the differences may require a lot of explanation, it would provide investors and analysts with far better information than they get today.

- *Core earnings.* Finally, a summary of core earnings would be the most revealing. This version would be the one used to project future growth in profits and capital strength.

Key Point

Reporting profits and losses realistically would represent real transparency. The big question should be: Why is this not happening?

Why is it unlikely that corporations will shift over to full transparency without a fight? The fact is, today's reporting environment is aimed at keeping stock prices as high as possible, so that institutional investors like mutual funds, insurance companies, and pension funds, will want to hold shares of stock. So the motivation is focused on stock price rather than on honest disclosures and corporate transparency. The corporate scandals hold important lessons for accountants, corporations, and securities analysts. Those lessons have not necessarily been learned. It is up to investors to find reality among the reported and often distorted numbers. The next chapter provides you with information you need to begin your search for financial reality beyond the audited financial statement.

Chapter 4

Finding Financial Information Online
Step-by-Step Explanations

The real problem is not whether machines think but whether men do.
—B. F. Skinner, *Contingencies of Reinforcement*, 1969

Getting financial information in the past was very cumbersome and time-consuming. Before the Internet, investors had to telephone or write to a corporation and request the latest annual report or financial statement; or they depended on a brokerage firm for the information.

Today, finding information online is easy, fast, and instant. It is simply a matter of going directly to corporate websites, clicking on the link (usually called "investor services" or "investor information"), and then opening up the latest financial statement. You will in this chapter see how this is done—step by step—for several sample corporations.

Having all financial information available online is a tremendous improvement in information compared to the past methods. One recurring complaint about fundamental information has always been that, by the time you conduct your review, the information is already out of date. While there is some truth to this, financial information continues to serve as the most reliable information on which to make investment decisions; and the Internet speeds up the access as well.

You can bypass the information lag by checking corporate websites regularly, tracking news and updates on your brokerage website and financial news websites, and reviewing interim reports corporations file with the SEC.

Selected Corporate Websites

To begin your review, locate the website for the corporation you want to analyze. In the previous chapter, several websites were included that provide free annual reports, and these will link you to the appropriate corporate sites. You can also find corporate home pages on your broker's site by entering the name, a partial name, or the trading symbol. Finally, the major stock exchanges also link to the *annual report* page for listed companies. While some of the "free" sites may ultimately assess a charge for their service, the exchange-linked annual reports are always free.

annual report
a publication released by listed companies to disclose to stockholders and regulators all of the relevant information about the company and its operations: markets and products, financial statements with footnotes, and summaries from the executive management of the company.

In the following list, you will find instructions for navigating through the websites of four well-known large corporations. Each example gives the approximate steps at the time of this writing to locate the latest free online copy of the corporation's annual report. You can use the same procedure to also find the most recent quarterly reports filed with the SEC or updates provided by the corporations for their investors.

General Electric (GE)—http://www.ge.com

1. Click Financial Reporting
2. Click Annual Reports
3. Then click on the latest annual report

IBM—http://www.ibm.com

1. Click About IBM
2. Click Investor Relations
3. Click Stockholder Resources
4. Then click Annual Report

JC Penney (JCP)—http://www.jcp.com.

1. Click About Us
2. Click Company Information
3. Click Investor Relations
4. Then click on the latest annual report

ExxonMobil (XOM)—http://www.exxonmobil.com

1. Click Investor Information
2. Click Featured Documents
3. Click on the latest annual report

The easiest way to locate web addresses for corporations is to refer to the free online sites, or to do a web search on the corporate name. A Google search on a corporate name will usually bring up the home page. All of the listed companies on the major exchanges can also be linked directly from the exchange home page. The following summarizes the use of exchange websites:

New York Stock Exchange—http://www.nyse.com

1. Click the listed company directory
2. Click on alphabetical subdirectory for the desired company
3. Click on company name
4. Then click on "website" link for the company

NASDAQ—http://www.nasdaq.com

1. Click Get free annual reports link at bottom of the page
2. Click Go to alphabetical subsection
3. Click on the corporation you are analyzing
4. Download the online version (usually a PDF File)

American Stock Exchange—http://www.amex.com

1. Click Links of interest: Annual report service
2. Navigate to alphabetical subsection
3. Click on the corporation you are analyzing
4. Download the online version (usually a PDF file)

These resources are free, easy to find, and convenient. You can even store copies of annual reports in your computer for those stocks that you own or are tracking as portfolio candidates.

Finding *and* Interpreting Key Facts

Once you have the information in hand, the next step is to decide exactly what information you will want to review. Future chapters provide you with detailed examples for all of the tests and ratios that you can perform on financial statements. The following is a review of the primary points of interest. These may be used to quick-check a company and, perhaps, to eliminate a company from your list of possible investments. For example, you may set some basic rules for yourself. You may decide to not invest in companies that have never shown a profit; those whose P/E ratio is too high; companies that do not pay dividends; or companies whose bonds are rated below investment grade. These are only examples of some of the elimination points you could employ. Here is a quick-checklist you can use to review the numbers as reported on the financial statements, without needing a detailed review:

1. *Comparison of sales, costs, expenses, and profits.* The most basic and obvious test is the test of earnings. Look at the statement of operations, not just for this year but for previous years as well. If the company has many divisions, look for breakdowns by operating unit (this is usually located in the footnotes). Also study the important attributes making up sales growth or decline. For example, in the retail sector, study the year-to-year changes in retail space and numbers of stores opened or closed. Are sales growing? And if so, are profits growing as well? The big danger signal is found when sales are flat or declining, but expenses keep rising; that is a sign of a poorly managed company. Even when sales are rising, if profits are falling at the same time, there could be problems.

   The sign of a well-controlled, well-managed company is one in which sales increase each year—not erratically but steadily—and costs remain at the same approximate percentage of sales. At the same time, expenses may be expected to rise somewhat during periods of growth, but not at the same rate as sales. Net profits should remain at approximately the same percentage of sales each year, while the dollar amount of net profits rises. That is the basic operating standard.

2. *Dividends declared and paid.* Corporations declare and pay dividends and those that raise their dividends each year also tend to be well-managed companies. This does not mean a company that does not pay dividends is not well managed; the dividend test is only one of many basic tests worth applying. You may also decide to limit your search to corporations that have increased their dividend every year. An excellent subscription service for those interested in tracking dividend records is Dividend Achievers (http://www.dividendachievers.com), a service published by Mergent Corporation. A quarterly publication lists those companies that have increased dividends for at least 10 years.

> Corporations with erratic earnings and large net losses cannot always afford to pay dividends because their cash flow tends to suffer along with the volatile earnings outcomes. A volatile operating record is a sign of problems, but companies with less *fundamental volatility* tend to also have better cash flow; consistent profits; and a better, more consistent dividend record.

3. *DRIPS program offered.* Rather than cash, many corporations allow stockholders to take dividends in additional partial shares. This is the most efficient way to reinvest dividends and achieve a compound rate of return. These *dividend reinvestment programs* (DRIPs) are valuable for anyone interested in accumulating value rather than receiving cash.

fundamental volatility

the degree of change from one year to the next in reported sales, costs, expenses, and earnings, as well as inconsistency in other fundamental trends, dividend payments, and ratio tests.

dividend reinvestment programs (DRIPs)

services provided by many corporations allowing stockholders to take dividends in additional partial shares instead of cash dividends. For example, if current share price is $75 per share and the quarterly dividend is $25, a DRIPs plan would allow the stockholder to acquire an additional one-third share.

Valuable Resource

For a complete listing of corporations offering DRIPs programs, check http://www.wall-street.com/directlist.html.

**price/
earnings ratio
(PE ratio)**

an important ratio
comparing the
current price per
share to the latest
known *earnings
per share* (EPS).
The PE multiple
summarizes the
market's percep-
tion about the
number of times'
earnings the
stock should be
worth, and it is a
combination of
both technical
(price) and funda-
mental (earnings)
information.

**earnings per
share (EPS)**

an important
fundamental indi-
cator, reflecting
net earnings each
year per outstand-
ing share. The
earnings are
divided by the
shares outstand-
ing to arrive at the
EPS, which is
reported in dollars
and cents.

4. *Price/Earnings (PE) ratio.* One of the most popular and interesting tests of a stock is the
price/earnings ratio (PE ratio). This is a comparison between the current price of a share of
stock to the latest known *earnings per share*
(EPS). The ratio is interesting because it compares a technical indicator (price) to a fundamental indicator (earnings per share). As a
general observation, when the PE is very high, it
indicates greater risk. As the multiple of earnings grows in the price, there is an increasing
chance that the market has overvalued the
stock. A midrange PE is usually found between
11 and 20, although opinions about "best" PE
level vary.

Many variations of price comparison are
used by analysts, and these are explained in detail in Chapter 9.

5. *Capitalization and debt ratio.* Easily overlooked
in the test of basic strength or weakness of a
company is the capitalization mix. A company's
total capitalization is the total of shareholders'
equity plus long-term debt. By definition, long-
term debt usually includes contracts, notes, and
bonds that take more than one year to repay.
The *debt ratio* is the percentage that long-term
debt represents of total capitalization. This is explored more in Chapter 7; but be aware of the
essential importance of a debt ratio trend: As
debt begins to represent more and more of total
capitalization, the trend becomes worse. It
means there will be less operating profit in the
future to fund operations and dividend payments because more cash will have to be used to
repay debts and to maintain interest payments
on those debts.

6. *Product or service and business sector.* What kinds of products or services are marketed and sold by the company? Are those products experimented, untested, and new? If so, the potential market will be unknown, which presents both risk and opportunity. Are the products currently going through a series of lawsuits? (For example, pharmaceutical companies may have exposure to expensive suits, threatening their profitability and capital safety.) Are the products or services potentially obsolete? When Polaroid filed for bankruptcy a few years ago, some people were surprised—but when you consider their product, it made sense. The "instant" camera was revolutionary in its day, but digital technology made the Polaroid camera obsolete. The company had not kept up with change.

total capitalization

the combination of long-term debt and shareholders' equity; the source of financing to fund corporate operations, consisting of debt and equity capital.

debt ratio

the portion of total capitalization represented by debt, as opposed to equity sources; when debt levels rise and corporations become less able to continue dividend payments or fund future operations.

    A critical analysis of what the company sells should include a comparative critique of how competitive it remains. Using the digital camera example, who is mastering that market today? With Hewlett-Packard, Xerox, and dozens of foreign corporations taking a market share, what is likely to happen to Kodak in the future? While Kodak has entered the market, they continue to consider old-style film their primary product. So what does this mean to you as a long-term investor? These are important questions to ask, and a comparative study of the corporations within a single industry can be revealing.

7. *Company position within the sector.* Each sector has a clear leader or two or three companies all vying for the lead in market share. The lead company may be quite large and well capitalized, but can it hold its lead indefinitely? What about second-tier corporations, the up and coming ones hungry for larger market share? These may be better long-term growth candidates, depending on the sector, the marketing strategy employed by each company, and the various capitalization sizes of companies. Some corporations try to offer everything to the market, whereas other competitors may specialize narrowly. This also affects future growth capabilities. The smaller corporations within a single sector may be undercapitalized to compete with the larger, stronger companies over the long term.

As a quick checklist, this is by no means a definitive fundamental analysis program; it is a starting point only. You do need to perform a detailed review, as you will find in coming chapters. As you review corporate financial reports, ask yourself some of the very basic questions as a means for deciding whether it is worth your time to investigate further. Here are three crucial questions you should ask:

1. *Has the company ever reported a profit?* It is virtually impossible to make judgments about a company on the basis of fundamental analysis if that company has never reported a profit. So many fundamental tests are comparative trends based on profitability. So many questions about management's effectiveness are also based on how well they maintain net profit from year to year; how growth affects profits; and how expansion of operating units diversifies the company's profits. If there has never been a profit, none of those essential tests can even be performed.

   It is amazing that during the dot.com Internet craze, so many companies without track records started up and attracted investors. Prices rose without fail over months and months, and investors continued pouring money into ever higher-priced stock. Many of those companies had never reported a profit. In fact, it was uncertain in some cases what those companies even sold. One important test of management's ability is the demonstrated ability to establish a reasonable level of profit and then to *repeat* that year after year, even as revenues grow.

2. *Can you follow a trend, or not?* Some corporations report a very erratic history of revenues, costs, expenses and profits. As a consequence, it is impossible to determine the long-term trend, because one has not been established. Other companies, by comparison, report steadily growing sales, consistent cost and expense levels, and predictable profits. This is a sign of good management. As an investor, you want to be able to estimate the direction the company is moving and predict its rate of growth.

High levels of fundamental volatility are a warning sign that management may be tinkering with its accounting policies or, at the very least, is not able to control expenses. Management is supposed to create a strategic marketing plan, track it from month to month, and generate revenues. At the same time, they are supposed to control costs and expenses. When this is done properly, the result is low volatility in the numbers. When management does not know how to control its forecasts and internal expenses, the result is high fundamental volatility.

3. *Are you looking for good investments or do you just like the company?* So many investors pick companies because they like the product without considering the relative value of the company as an investment. Many people hate Wal-Mart because they employ a smart, but ruthless marketing strategy. They offer lower prices than small local shops and, as a consequence, a lot of small businesses cannot compete. So as a potential investor, you need to make a distinction between personal feelings and investment value. It is a fact that, based on numerous fundamental tests, Wal-Mart is an excellent growth investment; Sears, by comparison, has been losing market share over many years. So you might like shopping at Sears and hate Wal-Mart. But that would not be a sound reason to buy Sears stock, which is fundamentally weak, and to reject Wal-Mart stock, which is fundamentally strong.

The same case applies to the selection of soft drinks, food companies, tobacco giants, computer software manufacturers, or recreation industry companies. If you do decide to invest on moral terms or on personal preferences for products, be aware of the underlying reasons for your choices. If you want to employ fundamental tests, it is important that you put aside personal preferences based on products or marketing strategies. The two do not mix well.

What Selected Financial Information Reveals

The purpose to analyzing annual reports is twofold. First, you need to confirm existing trends for stocks you are following or that you own. Second, you want to look for eliminating factors for stocks you are thinking of purchasing.

Every investor faces the dilemma of how to narrow down the list of potential investments. There are plenty of well-managed corporations to choose from, some with more risk than others, and some better managed than others. The range of indicators you choose to test also dictates how well you narrow the list. If your requirements are too stringent, you may find no stocks at all. If too loose, your list will be too long to enable you to make an informed decision.

Key Point

The purpose in narrowing down a list of potential investments is to avoid guesswork and to arrive at an informed decision.

portfolio management
a series of tests and monitoring procedures designed to ensure that a stock's fundamental strength remains; when that position changes, it may also be time to sell the stock.

When you already own stocks, analysis is part of your *portfolio management* task. It is never wise to buy stocks and then forget about them; and there is a tendency, even among fundamental investors, to watch price only. This is a mistake. Today's well-selected, fundamentally strong stock may change tomorrow, based on news and events, competitive changes, and the basic fundamental trends themselves.

Some of the areas worth monitoring include:

1. *News and developments.* The financial news often is uninteresting, but now and then an important story emerges that affects the fundamental value of your stock. For example, if a class action lawsuit is filed that could cost the company billions of dollars, that would certainly change its valuation. By the same argument, a corporation may receive a large contract. In the aerospace sector, a manufacturers' stock is invariably affected by large orders for planes but adversely affected by looming threats of strikes. News may not be restricted to business, either; it may be economic, political, or both, and the effect on a stock's value, at least in the short term, can be substantial.

   When news—good or bad—affects a company you own or are thinking of buying, the most important question to ask is: How does this affect long-term value of this company as an investment?

Of course, virtually everything is going to affect stock prices short-term, but most news does not change the long-term value of the company, so it should be discounted.

2. *Product announcements.* A similar impact on a company's value grows from product announcements. Some industries are more vulnerable to this than others. For example, FDA approval of a major new drug can boost a pharmaceutical company's value significantly, as well as its long-term value. If the FDA rejects a new drug, the opposite effect is seen; and if an existing drug is pulled from the market, lost revenues *and* the possibility of lawsuits also raise many questions concerning the value of the company for many years to come.

    Some industries are involved with research, and new product inventions or revisions will have a great impact on price. For years now there has been talk of developing alternate energy sources. If that ever comes to pass, would the current energy sector be a lead player in a new fuel technology market? Or would the sector suffer because it is heavily dependent on oil and gas? These kinds of questions surrounding products are complex. One sign of a company's vision is its ability to change with the times, branch out, diversify into new product areas, and anticipate obsolescence.

3. *Earnings surprises.* The favorite pastime on Wall Street is predicting and then comparing *earnings announcements.* Analysts predict quarterly earnings to the penny and then, when those earnings announcements are published, everyone compares the actual outcome to what the analysts predicted. Ironically, more weight is given to the prediction than to the actual outcome, and a difference of anything beyond a few pennies per share is an earnings surprise. But astute investors should question this system. What is the basis for the analysts' target for earnings? How did they arrive at it? Was it a fundamental or a technical estimate? Just as analysts set price targets, how is the earnings per share devised? If we do not know how the estimate was arrived at, then we cannot know how much validity to assign to it.

    A company may be very happy with its quarterly earnings, especially if those earnings exceed the previous period. However, if the analyst estimated a higher earnings than the company realizes,

earnings announcements

published summaries of quarterly earnings per share that a publicly traded corporation reports to the SEC. The announcement is used on Wall Street in comparison to analysts' earnings estimates.

Wall Street treats the outcome as negative news. The investing community is obsessed with technical indicators and short-term price movement and has little or no interest in financial information.

Key Point
Analysts' predictions about earnings are given more weight than actual outcome. Investors may rightfully wonder if these estimates were based on financial or technical information . . . and even on whether analysts understand how to interpret the fundamentals.

4. *Mergers and acquisitions.* Finally, be aware of how corporations merge with others or acquire smaller competitors. The acquisitions trend may be a positive or a negative factor. During the era of corporate scandals from 2001 to 2002, hindsight revealed that many of those corporations that ended up in trouble had been heavily acquiring others. The traditional view of acquisition has been that it eliminates competition, consolidates markets, and makes companies stronger. Rather than having to figure out how to capture added market share, companies have been viewed as buying that market share through mergers and acquisitions.

During the 1990s acquisitions took on a different face. The *roll-up strategy* used by many companies involved buying up hundreds of smaller corporations in the industry, often paying for them with stock. If a smaller company reports a net loss, those losses can be rolled into the short year of an acquisition (the "stub period") while revenues are deferred to the following full year. This has the result of inflating earnings, at least temporarily. One of the biggest cases of abusive reporting growing from big-volume acquisitions was Waste Management, Inc. During the 1990s it acquired hundreds of smaller companies and, according to SEC estimates, exaggerated its pretax profits by $1.43 billion. The company's auditors, Arthur Andersen, which approved the misleading financial reports, paid a $7 million fine and settled shareholder lawsuits for another $220 million.[1]

Paying for smaller companies with stock is inflationary, especially when the value is not there. It is a shell game and most of the corporations playing it ended up losing money and many even filed bankruptcy. It deceived investors, regulators, and accounting firms for years. If you notice a large volume of acquisitions on a financial report, the matter requires a closer look.

What Is Left Out of Financial Statements

Many articles, books, and online tutorials explain what is included on the financial statement, and in the annual report. But of equal importance and rarely discussed is what is *not* included. At times, the information that is left out can be more important than what is shown.

Disclosures about information not shown or explained well enough are supposed to be provided in the footnotes. But for nonaccountants, some of the note explanations are so cryptic and complex that they make no sense. So the solution may be to contact the company's *Shareholder Relations Department* and ask your question. In a responsive corporation, someone will return your call and explain the footnote to you. If you are thinking of investing in a company, one preliminary fundamental test worth making is telephoning the department and asking a question. The response will reveal whether future inquiries will be responded to satisfactorily, or whether the corporation does not have a service orientation.

It may be that finding the excluded information will be more difficult than interpreting what *is* there. Thus, many individuals working on their own will find this level of fundamental analysis to be time consuming as well as complicated. Two solutions should be considered: First, perform investment research with the expert help of a *financial planner*. Pick one who bases this research on experience and an understanding of the fundamentals, and who holds the professional designation *Certified Financial Planner* (CFP). It will cost money to hire a planner, but the benefits of expert selection may be

Shareholder Relations Department
a department within a publicly listed corporation set up specifically to address concerns and answer questions from shareholders. A test of corporate transparency and investor services is to test this department's response to financial questions.

financial planner

an individual with experience and credentials to advise investors on how to pick stocks and other products. A qualified planner should hold the CFP designation.

Certified Financial Planner (CFP)

a professional designation awarded to individuals who hold a BA degree, complete an education program, pass a 10-hour exam, and complete three years of experience in the field.

investment club

an informal organization of individuals who meet to share research chores, pool their money, and identify profitable investments; funds contributed by members are invested as a unit in the investments selected through the club members' research.

worthwhile. The second alternative is to organize or join an *investment club*. This is an organization of individuals, usually numbering between 10 and 20, who share research and meet regularly to discuss stocks and other investments. Usually firmly based in the fundamentals, investment clubs have proven to be successful forums for individuals who are not comfortable investing without consultation with others.

Valuable Resource

To find a qualified professional financial planner, check the website for the Financial Planning Association, at http://www.fpanet.org. Click "public / find a planner" to begin the process.

Valuable Resource

To find an investment club near you or to find out what is involved in forming your own club, vist the National Association of Investors Corporation (NAIC) website at http://www .betterinvesting.org.

Whether you work on your own or with professionals and fellow investors, you need to know what information is not shown on the financial statements. Some of the areas to remember are:

1. *Current market value of assets.* It is troubling that traditional accounting methods do not provide for accurate reporting of asset values. The balance sheet is supposed to summarize a company's equity value, but so many of the accounts on the balance sheet are inaccurate. One of these is the capital assets section. Many of these assets may be valued far higher or lower than the net value reported. A good example is real estate holdings. Under the accounting rules, buildings

are reported at their original purchase price; and that value declines each year because depreciation is claimed over time. This diminishing asset may, in fact, be increasing in market value and today's true value is likely to be far higher than the reported value.

The unreliability of the asset account is disturbing by itself. This also affects the book value of equity and as a result, the book value of stock. So, in essence, you are asked to decide whether today's price per share of stock is reasonable, even though the financial information you have available is outdated. The financial statement's footnotes may include an estimate of fair market value for real estate and other assets. If not, you may need to call the company and ask for more information.

2. *Current amount of unrecorded liabilities.* Just as the true value of assets is not reported on the balance sheet, many liabilities are simply left off; they are explained somewhere in the footnotes. Two major areas may be *lease commitments* and *pension liabilities.* A lease commitment is the liability owed to lease equipment or real estate. It exists under a contract so it is an actual liability; but under the accounting rules, lease commitments are not always required to be listed.

Of even greater concern is the unrecorded pension liability—that is, the amount the company is committed to pay retired employees, present and future, for their retirement benefits. In many corporations this is a huge liability and, were it recorded, the corporations would be bankrupt. General Motors, for example, owes more on its pension liability than its net worth. This is a disturbing shortcoming in the accounting and reporting rules, and the information can only be found in the footnotes.

3. *The potential liability known to the company from lawsuits.* Companies may be advised

lease commitments
liabilities under contract, often long-term, to pay rent for equipment, rights, or real estate. These liabilities are probably not recorded on the financial statement of a corporation and can only be found in the footnotes.

pension liabilities
the amount of money due to retired employees and accumulating in the accounts of current employees and due in the future. Pension liabilities are often substantial, but are normally not recorded on the balance sheet and can be found only in the footnotes to the financial statements.

contingent liability

a potential obligation that may or may not become an actual liability in the future, such as pending lawsuits filed against the company.

that lawsuits have been filed or are about to be filed against them. These may be individual or class action and, in many instances may end up costing the company millions or even billions of dollars. However, until a case is filed and either tried or settled, accounting rules do not require the company to list these as actual liabilities. Footnotes will disclose any *contingent liability* of this type, but they are not highlighted in the financial statements.

4. *Changes, if applicable, in accounting methods.* While accounting rules are complex and often confusing, some significant decisions might have been made that affect what you see on the financial statement. These may include methods for valuing inventory, accounts receivable and bad debt estimates and reserves, and other accounting matters.

   Trying to read the footnotes and understand (1) the nature of changes and (2) how they impact the profit or loss shown on the financial statement is not a simple matter.

5. *Impact of accounting decisions as to the timing that revenues, costs, or expenses have been recorded.* In addition to changes made in accounting methods, corporations may also have made decisions about the timing of reporting transactions. One of the more common practices in the widespread corporate scandals of the 1990s was the practice of prebooking revenues. Companies may simply make up the numbers, in which case it is outright fraud; but the smarter ones try to document a justification under the GAAP rules. There are numerous ways to "create" a justification for inflating revenues. First, revenues can be recorded although services are not going to be provided until later. Second, recording might occur before goods are shipped or orders accepted by customers. Third, revenues are booked even when customers have not actually placed orders, thus they are only estimates of *future* orders. Fourth, a corporation may book sales to its own subsidiaries or partners to create a higher dollar value.

All of these practices are deceptive. Even if corporations can get auditors to approve their timing of revenues improperly, it eventually comes around and leads to future adjustments. The same kind of adjustments may occur with costs and expenses. For example, expenses can be reduced by capitalizing them and writing them off over several years. This is not an especially imaginative technique, but it does increase reported profits this year. A more subtle approach is to change accounting methods so that some of this year's expenses are moved to a *previous* year. It is more subtle because, to appreciate the impact of this more subtle tinkering, you need to look at a series of financial statements. Many people simply ignore restated past statements, but this opens the possibilities up, especially for the creative accounting executive: Increasing this year's profits by moving expenses back in time to the previous year.

How to Ask Questions

Some of the troubling practices among corporate accounting professionals—often with the cooperation of so-called "independent" auditors—led to many misrepresentations in the 1990s and investigations in 2001 and 2002. Penalties, fines, even jail time and a new federal law have fixed only some of the problems. It remains important for every individual to investigate the reported information, look for problems, and ask questions.

Every corporation has its own Shareholder Relations Department, designed to respond to your questions, ensure transparency, and when necessary to forward your questions to the right department for response. If something on the financial statement is not clear, an inquiry to the Shareholder Relations Department should lead to a prompt answer—either from the department directly or from someone else within the company. As a simple test of investor relations and the quality and timing of response, this is an excellent starting point. A corporation that provides prompt, accurate answers is, at the very least, making an effort to work with its investors to improve the lines of communication.

Besides the complexity of simply finding the information you need, it is also essential to test the accuracy of the numbers. In this chapter a limited explanation of revenue and expense adjustments was introduced. However, there is much more to it. In the next chapter, you will see the many ways that corporations present inaccurate information and learn how to spot the various kinds of adjustments that have been made.

Chapter 5

How Accurate Are the Numbers?

We must always remember that market research, no matter how well done, is based on the past. We are always susceptible to discovering a truth whose time has gone.
—Mark A. Johnson, *The Random Walk and Beyond*, 1988

The expression *cookie jar accounting* refers to a practice some companies engage in: moving profits from this year to the future. So if current revenues and profits are exceptionally high, some profits are put into the cookie jar and reported in a future year when revenues and profits are comparatively low. This is also called *sugar bowl accounting*.

To some people, this practice is acceptable because it smoothes out otherwise volatile results and provides a more predictable trend. Investors prefer low-volatility, highly predictable results in their investments. But because the practice is not accurate, it is also wrong. It masks a very real problem: a tendency for year-to-year results to be volatile. It would be a more accurate type of reporting to show the *real* numbers in each year and allow analysts and investors to figure out why the volatility exists. It may be economic or

> **cookie jar accounting**
> the practice of moving profits from an exceptionally high-profit year to a future relatively low-profit year in order to even out the reported revenues and profits. Also called *sugar bowl accounting*.

sugar bowl accounting

movement of reported totals from high-profit years to future low-profit years in order to even out reported operating results. Also called *cookie jar accounting*

market-oriented, or it may occur because management is not properly planning and controlling its own marketing. Either way, whenever current operating results are artificially moved to another period, it is a problem.

Some people also believe that it is acceptable to move profits forward because that provides a cushion for the future; and at the same time, it would not be acceptable to inflate current earnings and absorb the overage in future periods. Realistically, however, both decisions involve manipulation of results and should be disallowed.

Key Point

Some believe it is acceptable to move profits ahead but not to overstate profits this year. Both are deceptive practices—and both hide the facts you need to make informed decisions.

Accountants within the corporate structure, and auditors reviewing the books, know that GAAP provides enough flexibility to allow some questionable movement of profits. The flexibility of GAAP is itself a serious problem. The general "rule of thumb" within the accounting industry is that decisions to move profits from one year to another are all right as long as there is a documented justification. This is unfair to investors because it represents intentional distortion of the results, done under the guise of GAAP. Consider the following fictional example of an explanation accompanying the deferral of sales and profits to a future period:

Revenues and associated costs, expenses and net profits, reduced for the purpose of deferring for estimated current-period and reported results estimated to belong properly to next year's revenues, costs and expenses; based on assumed preordering from major customers for inventory to be applied to customers' future-year activity and in anticipation of lower than normal levels of future orders to be placed.

This explanation justifies the movement of current-year profits, essentially arguing that this year's orders were exceptionally high and, therefore, it may be that the following orders will be lower because customers are stocking up. However, even if this is an accurate observation, it is not justification for moving profits forward. A basic rule in accounting is that all transactions are supposed to be reported in the proper year. Moving transactions forward based on a belief about ordering volatility is not accurate.

Some Accounting Principles: Accruing Transactions

Accountants use *journal entries* to adjust the books, and a wide variety of reasons justify these adjustments. For example, they may be used to fix previous account coding errors; to set up transactions made in this period that do properly apply later; and to report liabilities that have not yet been paid.

> **journal entries**
> adjustments made to the books and records to correct errors, report transactions that belong in the current period but that have not yet occurred, to move transactions to later periods when they occur too soon, and to record noncash transactions.

Key Point
Accounting is complex and requires expertise to manage. The problem is not merely in its complexity, but in the degree to which its nature invites abuse.

The big problem with the complexity of accounting procedures is that it invites abuse. There are good reasons to make journal entries, as described in the following list; but this also means that the legitimate reasons to make adjustments can easily lead to manipulation and misrepresentation of operating results. Listed here are typical reasons for journal entries followed by examples of how these have been abused in the past and how you can protect yourself by recognizing questionable adjustments. The common types of journal entry adjustments include:

1. *Reporting income earned but not yet received.* The typical accounting system depends on the *accrual* of noncash transactions. An accrual is a journal entry made to book income that has been earned in the current period but not yet received, or costs and expenses incurred but not yet paid. When something is placed into

accrual

a system in accounting of booking revenues, costs, and expenses prior to cash exchanging hands; the purpose is to book these in the proper accounting period. It often occurs that cash transacts later than the period income is earned or expenses are incurred.

recognition

in accounting the process of booking revenues and costs and expenses in the proper period, even when cash has not yet traded hands. The purpose of recognizing items early is to make the reported books accurate in order to include not only cash but earned income and incurred costs and expenses.

the books to report it in the current period, it is called *recognition* in the accounting business. The transaction is "recognized" and thus reflected so that the current period books are accurate.

Key Point

It is the timing of recognition—the year in which revenues and costs and expenses are booked—that determines overall profitability. Because accountants make these decisions, they have the power to manipulate; and that power is sometimes abused.

A corporation may report a large sale near the end of the year. However, the customer has not yet paid the bill for the goods that were delivered; payment is expected to occur within 30 days, which will place the cash transaction in the following year. To ignore this *earned income* would be unrealistic, because it was earned in the current year. So a journal entry is prepared to recognize the income in the current year. Because cash will not be received until later, the offsetting entry is made to *accounts receivable*, a current asset. Later, when cash is received, the balance of accounts receivable will be reduced. The net effect is that income is booked in the proper period; cash is booked when received; and accounts receivable has one entry going in and an offsetting entry coming back out.

2. *Reporting expenses not yet paid.* Just as income may be earned in advance of cash receipt, costs and expenses can be incurred. For example, a corporation orders supplies this month, but is not invoiced until later. To accurately recognize the expense in the current month, it needs to make a journal entry. The appropriate cost or expense category has an entry made, offset by an equal amount to the current liability account, *accounts payable*. Later,

when payment is made, an offsetting entry is made to remove the liability and to show a reduction in the cash account. The total of these *accrued expenses* reflects the currently owed amounts.

The procedure for entering accruals of income, costs, and expenses is done by way of journal entry. A *debit* and a *credit* are entered for each and every transaction in the *double-entry bookkeeping* system in every instance; the sum of all debits and all credits is always zero, meaning the books are in balance. It is not accurate to think of a debit as a plus and a credit as a minus; the use of "plus" and "minus" values is done as a control feature, and both sides of every entry are equally important.

A summary of accruals and the debit and credit entries involved for income, costs, and expenses is shown in Figure 5.1.

Note in the figure that the entries are designed to show all operating entries (income and costs and expenses) in the current period, while cash is received or paid later. So the accounts receivable and accounts payable values are always entered and then reversed. This system enables accountants to accurately reflect the earned income and incurred costs and expenses in the proper period, while cash transactions often occur later.

earned income
revenues earned in one period and properly reported in that period even if actual payment will not occur until later; to report income accurately, earned income is entered by way of a journal entry, offset by an addition to the current asset, accounts receivable.

accounts receivable
a current asset consisting of balances due from customers, used to report earned income in the proper accounting period even when cash will not be received until later.

accounts payable
a current liability reflecting all of the currently owed costs and expenses; the account is used to recognize costs and expenses in a current period even though they will not be paid until later.

Key Point
The purpose of accruals is to ensure that all earned income and incurred costs and expenses are reported in the proper period—but this is not always how accruals are used.

	Current Period	Future Period
Income Earned	Debit Accounts Receivable Credit Revenue	Debit Cash Credit Accounts Receivable
Costs and Expenses Incurred	Debit Cost or Expense Credit Accounts Payable	Debit Accounts Payable Credit Cash

FIGURE 5.1　Accrual Entries

**accrued
expenses**

those expenses that are payable but not yet paid, representing currently incurred obligations that will be billed by invoice or statement in the future, usually in the following month.

debit

a left-sided entry and part of equal debits and credits in all instances as part of a double-entry bookkeeping system; the purpose of debits and credits is to ensure that the books are always in balance.

3. *Adjusting current books for income received in advance.* The most common occurrence requiring accruals is when revenues earned this period will not be paid until later. The reverse can occur as well. In some cases a customer may make payment before the period the income is earned. Any revenue received in advance of the period when it is earned is properly classified as *deferred income*. A corporation, for example, receives an order for goods to be shipped in two months; however, the customer advances a partial payment. In this case the payment is a deposit, perhaps made to secure the order. It should be treated as being earned in a future period; an entry is made involving a debit to the cash account and a credit in the liability section of the balance sheet. Although the receipt is not technically a liability, it is entered there as a deferred credit. Conceivably, if the order were to be cancelled, the deposit may be returned to the customer. It would be inaccurate, however, to book prepaid revenues as being earned in the current period.

4. *Adjusting current books for expenses paid in advance.* The need to make adjustments for expenses paid in advance is quite common. Remember, the purpose to making journal entries is to reflect current revenues and costs and expenses in the proper period. When *prepaid expenses* occur, a portion has to be set up as an asset. Each month, a portion is moved from the asset account to the expense account—this is a process called *amortization*.

It is common practice, for example, to prepay insurance policies. A premium for a full year may be payable in advance two-thirds of the way through a *fiscal year* of a company. In this case one-third is applicable to the current year and two-thirds to the following year. So two-thirds of the payment will be set up as a prepaid expense and reversed in the following year.

credit
a right-sided entry and part of equal debits and credits in all instances as part of a double-entry bookkeeping system; the purpose of debits and credits is to ensure that the books are always in balance.

double-entry bookkeeping
the system of entering transactions in the books and records of a company, whether consisting of cash or accruals; all entries consist of a left-sided debit and a right-sided credit. The two sides always contain equal value, so that the control feature is designed to guarantee mathematical accuracy. The sum of all debits and all credits should always be zero.

Key Point

Relatively simple concepts like management of prepaid assets often lead to mischief among corporate accounting departments. It is accurate to say that problems begin with minor decisions, and that the devil *is* in the details.

---

5. *Adjusting current books to anticipate future losses.* Another type of journal entry is one made to set up reserves for future estimated losses. For example, the current asset called *accounts receivable* is the total of money due from customers; some portion of accounts receivable will become *bad debts* in the future and will not be collectible. Each year the total of accounts receivable is reduced to set up an entry to a *reserve for bad debts*.

deferred income

any income received in the current period but not earned until a future period; this is properly set up as a deferred credit in the liability section of the balance sheet, to be reversed later when the revenue becomes earned (for example, when goods are shipped to the customer).

prepaid expenses

those expenses paid in advance and set up as prepaid assets to be amortized over a period of months; the result is to reflect the expense in the proper periods.

amortization

writing down an account over a period of time—such as when a prepaid asset is gradually amortized so that the expense is reported in the applicable month and year.

This appears as a reduction of the current asset. It is appropriate because, even though it is an estimate, the effort has to be made to recognize these bad debts in approximately the same year they are established to make the books as accurate as possible. An entry is made to debit the bad debt expense account and to credit the reserve for bad debts; each year, the estimate is adjusted based on actual experience.

6. *Adjustments for noncash expenses.* Most transactions of a company eventually end up in cash form. Even a large volume of accruals are made to manage timing differences; those current asset and liability account entries are normally reversed the following year. However, some journal entries are made for items that will not occur in the form of cash. For example, if an expense is assigned to the wrong account, a journal entry is used to make a correction. Various adjustments may be required from time to time to adjust errors such as these. One major expense occurs without any cash exchanging hands. Capital assets are set up on the balance sheet, and periodic expenses for *depreciation* are entered. This is a periodic *write-off* of a portion of the asset. For example, automobiles are depreciated in only a few years, while buildings take three decades. Land cannot be depreciated at all. So various rules govern how depreciation is calculated. An entry is made in each accounting period (month, quarter, or year) to show the expense (a debit) and an offsetting reduction in the long-term asset (a credit called accumulated depreciation). Eventually, at the end of the depreciable period, the total of accumulated depreciation will equal the original depreciable base of the asset (usually the original cost).

The Basic Reporting Problem: Inaccuracy

All of the valid types of journal entries serve legitimate purposes in the accounting system. However, they also can be misused. Journal entries within the accrual system can be applied to control currently reported revenues, costs, and expenses to achieve a desired result. So in years of exceptionally high income, earnings can be deferred to a following year. This reduces tax liabilities and allows the company to smooth out its reported earnings. Showing lower volatility in the numbers is desirable because it creates an illusion of predictability and consistency.

There is a problem. Using the accrual system in that way is deceptive. Investors and analysts have every right to see volatility and even chaos within the reported results. In many industries short-term competitive activity is highly chaotic and volatile. So when a company reports remarkable consistent revenues, costs, and expenses year after year, it should raise a question: Are the operating results correctly entered from one year to the next?

Key Point

Everyone likes predictability. Investors feel safe when they see sales and profits rising steadily each year. Too much consistency and too much predictability, however, could mean that some degree of manipulation is taking place.

Consistency at the expense of accuracy is a false indicator. Even if a company is able to manipulate the books so that everyone is satisfied with the gradual growth in revenues and the strong net earnings, it remains troubling if those results are based

fiscal year
the corporate 12-month period used for closing the books and reporting taxes as well as annual financial statements. A fiscal year does not always correspond to a calendar year, but may end on any month of the corporation's choosing, often set based on natural market and economic cycles.

bad debts
accounts receivable carried on the corporate books as a current asset that will become uncollectible in the future. A reserve is set up to estimate bad debts likely to occur based on receivables booked each year.

reserve for bad debts
an account shown in the current assets section of the balance sheet reducing accounts receivable. It represents an estimate of future bad debts based on current accounts receivable levels.

depreciation
a noncash expense reflecting periodic value of capital assets. All capital assets (except land) are fully depreciated over a period of years, involving regular annual allowances (straight-line depreciation) or larger write-offs in the earlier years and lower write-offs later (accelerated depreciation). All capital assets except land are depreciated over several years.

write-off
the process of reducing an asset's value and converting it to an expense. This occurs when an asset becomes valueless or, in the case of capital assets, through recording of periodic depreciation.

on less than reliable accounting policies. Is this a fine point only? No; in fact, the corporate scandals that were practiced throughout the 1990s and publicized in 2001 and 2002 were invariably generated through accounting adjustments. It is unlikely that all instances of manipulation started out with intentional misrepresentations; such things tend to grow in small steps.

Motivation for these practices often was a cause. Corporate executives often are paid for keeping the stock price high and for delivering exceptional operating results. With incentive compensation (bonuses and stock options, for example) often in the multi-millions of dollars, some CEOs and CFOs gave in to temptation and made decisions to alter the books. For a while, the board of directors, Wall Street analysts, and auditors were all happy, because the results were excellent. Even the Dow Jones Corporation liked Enron enough to add the company to its prestigious averages before the whole deception came to light. This demonstrates how easily even the experts in the industry can be fooled. If nothing else, every investor should be aware of the flaws in GAAP and of how easily the numbers can be manipulated within the rules.

The inaccuracy of reporting, even after the well-known corporate frauds that came to light a few years ago, remains a serious problem for every investor. To manage the problem of inaccuracy, follow these guidelines:

1. *Rely on the fundamentals.* The basic rule of thumb is to keep your eye on the financial results. Do not give in to the temptation to make trading decisions based on price movements or on rumor and short-term news. The financial results are the most trustworthy source for making investment decisions. Knowing that the numbers can be manipulated and misrepresented remains a chronic problem; but identifying the proper trend analysis tools

will help you to identify suspicious trends and to make decisions cautiously—or avoid companies with puzzling numbers.

2. *Look for consistency in the long term.* It is long-term results that demonstrate whether a corporation is able to manage its operating results and markets. Manipulation occurs only for a few years and, eventually, any artificially inflated results have to be absorbed. So when you see trends that are new and have not been established for many years, they cannot be used as reliably as trends lasting many years.

3. *Be suspicious of rapid and exceptional growth.* Many of the problems coming out of the years of corporate fraud were sudden and dramatic. Any fundamental investor should be suspicious when growth is unusually rapid and sustained. It simply is unlikely for growth to occur that way. Growth tends to occur consistently and gradually over many years. So a short burst of high earnings may be the result of liberal accounting policies, exaggerated accruals, and even outright fraud. With new federal laws designed to make such fraud more difficult, it is less likely. But it is virtually certain that fraud will not disappear altogether. Investors should remain suspicious when reported results look too good to be true.

4. *Be suspicious of high fundamental volatility.* It is very troubling to fundamental analysts when year-to-year results are volatile. It makes any type of long-term prediction difficult. Volatile financial results can also be a sign of excessive accounting tinkering. There are varying degrees of policy within companies. Some organizations have a very liberal interpretation of accounting rules, and the result often is a high volume of nonrecurring charges, adjustments, and restatements of past results. The more of this you see, the more suspicious you should be.

5. *Remember, prices do not rise forever.* Even the most dedicated fundamental investor is susceptible to temptation. When a stock's price climbs dramatically, many people want to buy shares and cash in on the trend; this is speculative and you must remember that the highest level of buying occurs at the highest price. A stock's price is not going to rise forever. Everyone knows this, but during the past decade it was easy to overlook the obvious truth. Thousands of investors lost millions of dollars putting too much

value in the short-term trends of dot.com companies such as Amazon, Yahoo!, eBay, and others. Thousands more lost money in WorldCom, Enron, Tyco, and even Xerox, all of which were scrutinized due to questionable accounting practices. Stay with the fundamentals, follow the trends, and be suspicious when things change. More than anything else, remember that short-term trends—especially on the technical side—are not reliable as indicators, and should not be used to determine when to buy, hold, or sell.

Why Year-to-Year Comparisons Are Difficult

In theory, the basic idea is a sound one: Compare financial statements from one year to the next to see how operating results have changed. Sales should continue to grow, costs should remain at the same percentage of revenues, and expenses should change very little. If this continues, earnings will rise each year.

Key Point

Annual comparisons are rarely simple. Due to a variety of changes in the very structure of a corporation, this year's results are often not comparable to last year's without making some type of adjustment.

That is the theory. Tracking fundamental trends in practice from one year to the next is more complex. It is likely that you will need to adjust even your long-term trend analysis to reflect adjustments, even when no questionable manipulation is involved. This is due to the need to restate prior years' earnings.

For example, a corporation may sell off one of its major operating units in the current year. So any year-to-year trends you follow have to be adjusted to remove previous earnings for that operating unit. Now that future growth will exclude the sold-off unit, it would be inaccurate to compare new results to previous trends. This occurred in the case of Altria, which sold off its Miller Brewing segment in 2002. A trend following revenues each year would have to be adjusted to remove Miller Brewing revenues, or the consolidated results would be inaccurate. The effect of Miller's revenues was substantial as shown in Table 5.1:

TABLE 5.1	Miller Brewing's Revenues (in millions)		
Year	Altria Total	Miller	Net
2000	$73,503	$4,907	$68,596
2001	80,879	4,791	76,088
2002	80,408	2,641	77,767

Source: Historical results, http://www.altria.com.

The year of the sale reported lower revenues than usual for Miller Brewing because the unit was sold in the middle of the year. This case is a good example of why results used in historical trend analysis may have to be adjusted. On average, more than 6 percent of annual revenues were earned from the Miller Brewing unit; so once it had been sold, using unadjusted historical revenue numbers would be very inaccurate.

Adjustments to previous results are essential for development of reliable trends. The need for such adjustments arises from the sale of an operating unit (whether it produces a significant profit or loss); or as the result of acquisitions and mergers. If corporations merge and report their consolidated revenues and costs and expenses, you have a double problem. First, the historical results are no longer reliable for trend analysis without restatement. Second, the new mix of business on a consolidated basis may be substantially altered.

For example, in some industries, gross profit (revenues minus costs, profit before expenses) may be quite high. Companies like Microsoft and IBM, for example, report significantly different levels of gross profit. Investors may consider both of these corporations as "computer" industry members. Microsoft's revenues, however, are derived predominantly from software sales and IBM's come mostly from hardware sales. Gross profit in Microsoft is substantially greater than IBM's as a result. So any time a corporation merges with another, the consolidated results may represent an averaging of disparate product lines. Those lines may exhibit vastly different financial results and trends. So in continuing to follow operating results through trends, it is important to review the operating segments separately; or to revise the entire review process based on the postacquisition mix of business and restatement of past results.

> **Key Point**
>
> Although restatements often have sound justifications, a record of frequent changes in accounting policy should raise many questions.

Restatements occurring as the result of changes in accounting policy are troubling and complex. It occurs from time to time that corporations make a decision to change the way they value inventories, calculate bad debt reserves, or otherwise change their accounting. This means that past results should be restated to reflect those changes as well. Otherwise, the trends are unreliable and your assumptions will be wrong. Whenever you see nonrecurring one-time adjustments occurring in several subsequent years, treat it as a red flag. Constant adjustments and readjustments could be an early warning sign that the results are being manipulated to inflate the numbers.

Complexity versus Fraud

Most investors accept the unavoidable complexity of financial reporting. It is a very difficult science and many estimates are involved. However, it is equally important to be able to make a distinction between complexity and fraud.

front-end load

an accounting term referring to the practice of recognizing revenues too early; a deceptive accounting decision to inflate current earnings by overstating revenues.

There are at least six common ways that accounting has been used to alter financial results using the accrual system and creative accounting. You need to be aware of all of these, because they can be used to distort the picture of what is really going on in a company:

1. *Recording revenues before they are earned.* In the recent past, some corporations have been found practicing what accountants call *front-end load* of revenues. This means that in one way or another, current operating results are distorted because revenues were recorded too early.

Key Point
One big problem with early booking of revenues is that it is deceptive. Another is that at some point in the future, the exaggeration has to be absorbed; that often means big losses and drastic declines in stock prices . . . not to mention possible legal problems for corporate executives and accountants.

There are three specific practices that corporations have used to accomplish this excessive report of revenues. It is fairly uncommon to simply create revenues out of nothing; the more creative approach is to interpret the rules favorably, even though inaccurately. The most obvious form is to recognize revenues before any services have been provided, often to existing customers and based on past ordering trends. The second practice is to record revenues as belonging in the current accounting period before goods are shipped or before customers even accept the conditions of a sale. The third is to record revenues when there has been no actual sale, often in cases where advance orders exist but have not yet been committed to by customers.

More sophisticated versions of early booking of revenues may include artificial creation of sales. For example, a corporation may generate "sales" to its subsidiaries, operating units, or partners. Some aggressive techniques have also included booking of sales when, in fact, a deal was made with customers to barter, exchange, or offset the cost of accepting goods. The accounting rules clearly specify that revenues should be recorded only upon completion of the earnings procedures and only when the customer is specifically obligated to make payment. Sales between a corporation and an "affiliated party" are not legitimate.

Among well-known corporations that were caught abusing the rules were Sunbeam, which, beginning in 1996, recorded revenues for gas grills as long as six months before the market season began. Big discounts were offered to retailers to take early delivery, even though actual delivery would not occur for many months to come. The exaggerated revenues were $29 million.

percentage of completion (POC)

a method of accounting in which revenues are recognized periodically based on the degree of job completion; used by construction and similar industries, POC is an estimate intended to recognize earnings during a lengthy process.

nonrecurring gains

any gain from the sale of capital assets, reclassified balance sheet accounts, or other adjustments that may distort the financial picture unless they are removed from the trend analysis.

The question of when to book revenues is not always this clear-cut, however. In some industries, such as construction, aerospace, and other industries involving a lengthy completion term, a method called *percentage of completion* (POC) accounting is used and for good reason. Revenues are supposed to be recognized based on the percentage a job has been finished. In some cases, however, POC has been used by companies that should not be employing the method; and in other cases, the percentage itself has been exaggerated to inflate current-year revenues.

2. *Reporting nonrecurring gains.* A corporation may easily exaggerate the true operating picture by reporting nonrecurring earnings. For example, if a corporation sells capital assets, it realizes a one-time profit. But for anyone trying to track fundamental trends, these *nonrecurring gains* should be excluded from the analysis.

The distortions in such items are often found in corporations losing market share in their primary business. To bolster the trends, the nonrecurring items are booked in a year so that some analysts will fail to look closely enough to see what is being done. In 1976 General Electric acquired its largest subsidiary at the time, Utah International. Because the purchase was accomplished with an exchange of GE stock, GE ended up overstating income as a result of the transaction. Because this exchange was nonrecurring, it should not have been considered as part of an analysis of GE's long-term earnings. A similar distortion occurred in the case of Boston Chicken, which was losing ground in its primary business of franchise fees and restaurant business. Its earnings were inflated with interest income; but with help from investment banker Merrill Lynch, Boston Chicken was able to attract investors from 1993 through 1996. The distorted reports masked the problem until 1996, when the company reported a net loss of $156 million. The company filed bankruptcy in 1998. But the point is, investors were deceived for more than four years because the numbers were inflated artificially.

Key Point

Including one-time profits in annual reports as part of a pattern is unrealistic and misleading. Even so, corporations do this every year and, unfortunately, many industry analysts seem oblivious to the inaccuracy it creates.

Generally speaking, companies are supposed to highlight capital gains separately from the reported *operating* income. In this way, analysts can see the difference and focus on operational net profit rather than overall profits that include nonrecurring profits. But some companies have tried to hide nonrecurring profits by using such one-time gains to reduce expenses (thus, artificially bolstering net operating profit). In 1999, IBM sold a unit to AT&T and rather than reporting it separately, simply reduced its operating and selling expenses, making it impossible to find the gain anywhere on IBM's financial statement.

3. *Deferring current-year expenses to another period or capitalizing expenses.* Just like revenues, expenses are supposed to be reported and recognized in the applicable accounting period. This is a basic accounting rule. But it is all too easy to defer expenses to a future period, setting them up as "prepaid" or "deferred" assets and amortizing them over time (even when they are not truly prepaid assets). Even more difficult to find is capitalization of expenses. This involves setting up a block of expense as a capital asset and depreciating that block over several years. These practices are deceptive because they artificially distort the current year's earnings.

It is relatively easy to find expenses that are artificially set up for future write-off. It is more difficult to find a block of expenses assigned to an earlier year, and that year's results restated. These types of adjustments may slip through the cracks and their impact never really known.

For example, AOL capitalized marketing expenses for the years 1995 to 1996. They gave these expenses the fancy name, "deferred membership acquisition costs" and treated them as assets to be amortized over a two-year period. The distortion was substantial. A reported $21 million loss in 1995 would have been $98 million if properly recorded. In 1996 the numbers were even worse. The reported loss of $62 million (before taxes) should have been $175 million. So shareholders were deceived by the deceptive practice.

Key Point

Manipulating profits by reducing expenses prevents you from seeing and identifying poor management. That is the real problem; the financial deception is just one of the symptoms of a more serious problem.

A more subtle distortion resulted from accounting practices at Snapple, the beverage company. Its marketing expenses virtually evaporated when the company decided they belonged to an earlier year. In 1994, Snapple made an accounting change in which estimates were used to set up expense reserves each year. So due to the accounting change, $1.6 million of 1994 were reclassified as properly belonging to earlier years. Caught in the deception, Snapple's exaggerated profits led to significant loss in share value and, late in 1994, Snapple was bought by Quaker Oats.

Amortizing costs too slowly is another variation of improper expense deferral. Cineplex Odeon tried writing off its leasehold improvements in theaters over 27 years rather than the more reasonable standard of 15 years. The result was an exaggerated earnings picture in 1988. Orion Pictures had a similar questionable practice, amortizing its film costs over too long a period and exaggerating current profits as a result.

A related problem arises when companies do not write off valueless assets or write down impaired assets. In other words, once an asset loses value, a loss should be taken to accurately reflect that value on the books. In the 1970s, Lockheed began developing its TriStar L-1011 program. By 1975, the deferred cost write-offs sat at $500 million, but the TriStar program was showing no signs of turning a profit. Lockheed's decision to write off this asset over 10 years was unrealistic and, by 1981, the asset had grown to over $1 billion. So annual profits were exaggerated each year until 1981, when Lockheed finally acknowledged the problem and took a one-time write-down of $400 million. The same types of misrepresentations can result from undervalued reserves for bad debts, inflated value of obsolete inventory, and similar assets being carried on the books as values far above realistic levels. Lucent Technologies, for example, was able to boost reported earnings by tinkering with its inventory reserves levels. Its earnings were exaggerated by $36 million in one quarter of 1999.

4. *Nonreporting of off-balance sheet liabilities.* Most people assume, when they see a financial statement, that everything has been reported. The statement is supposed to be a complete summary of all of a corporation's transactions and, in the case of the balance sheet, all of its assets and liabilities.

Key Point

All of the transactions and accounts of a corporation show up on the financial statements, right? Think again. Among the more serious problems with the way accounting is performed is what is *not* shown on the financial disclosures.

Most balances sheets exclude contingent liabilities, disclosing them only in obscure footnotes. So pending lawsuits, and the potentially large losses that they may incur, are not going to be found in the liability section of the balance sheet. Long-term leases and purchasing agreements are also not recorded even when they represent a significant liability. Most troubling of all is the approval of such practices by the accounting industry and its ill-defined GAAP system.

The problem goes beyond the contingent liability and long-term lease obligations. In fact, some corporations have been even more blatant, failing to even record expenses and their related liabilities in the proper year. Changes in accounting may also result in reducing liability values. Reserve values may also be lowered, resulting in lower liabilities offset by exaggerated income. Finally, a corporation might record revenues in the current year, but fail to also record related liabilities for costs and marketing expenses related to the revenues. All of these practices exaggerate profits and earnings per share, providing investors with a false picture of the value in their companies.

One huge example from the recent past was a failure by most corporations to record expenses and related liabilities for incentive stock options granted to executives and employees. The numbers are huge and, while accounting rules have been modified, the transition is gradual and underreported liabilities remain in many instances. Cisco's earnings would have been reduced by $1.1 billion in fiscal 2001—42 percent of reported earnings—if its expense options had been included. If Microsoft had expensed stock options in 1998, its reported $4.5 billion profit would have been reduced to a $17.8 billion loss. Many corporations, including Microsoft, have stopped granting stock options; others, such as General Electric, have begun recording the liability even as the slow-moving GAAP system has begun amending the accounting standards concerning stock options. This and many other problems remain concerning unrecorded liabilities.

5. *Deferring current-year revenues to the future.* The most common form of sugar bowl or cookie jar accounting involves the fairly simple technique of deferring current-year revenues to a future year. Some people believe that deferring revenues or profits is acceptable, whereas exaggerating current revenues or profits is not. As far as investors are concerned, any misrepresentation about each year's properly recognized earned income and incurred costs or expenses is wrong and should be treated under the same standard. Deferring revenues is problematical because, if allowed during profitable years, why should a corporation not also be allowed to exaggerate revenues when times are slow?

Key Point

The attempt on the part of corporations to smooth out earnings may appear well intended. But it is a bigger problem than it may seem because it eliminates fundamental volatility, and you should know about that.

The technique is accomplished in two specific ways. First, current-year reserves are set up, with plans to release these reserves in the future when the revenues are needed to bring profits up to a trend-based standard. Second, revenues earned this year are not even recognized until a future period; any receipts are set up as deferred credits or called "unearned" income and pushed forward to the next year.

W. R. Grace, well-known chemical giant, had a big surge in revenues in the early 1990s due to policy changes in the Medicare system. The company set up reserves that exceeded $50 million by 1992. Steady increases in earnings between 23 and 37 percent were reported from 1991 to 1995, which look impressive. However, actual growth was far more volatile, so investors and analysts were deceived. The SEC uncovered the activity and sued the company.

A practice even more aggressive was discovered at Microsoft. In 1998 and 1999, the company set up billions in reserves to defer revenues. Unearned revenues, as the reserves were called, exceeded $4 billion by the end of 1999. The experience of both W. R. Grace and Microsoft reveal that attempting to smooth out reported earnings through establishment of fictitious reserves not only deceives stockholders; ultimately, it also affects the stock price when the deception becomes known.

6. *Recording future expenses as current-year expenses.* Deferring revenues to even out long-term reported earnings is a troubling practice because, as many people believe, it is relatively benign. However, distortion prevents you from seeing the true picture; so it should be considered equally troubling as practices involving an exaggeration of current earnings. Setting up reserves or recording revenues as deferred credits is fairly easy to spot. Much more difficult is the practice of recording expenses before they are incurred. This practice is less visible, but it has the same affect as deferring revenues. By reducing future expenses, corporations control and equalize reported earnings per share. Once a corporation begins tinkering with the timing of expense recognition, it becomes increasingly difficult to tell what is really occurring from year to year.

> ### Key Point
>
> Some companies have been called on putting off revenues. A solution has been to artificially increase current-year expenses instead. We should not forget that this is another, more creative version of the same deceptive practice.

Unjustified prerecorded expenses are uncovered by analyzing expense levels from year to year. A well-managed company should report fairly consistent levels of expenses each year, with expected increases as sales volume grows; but the relative expense levels should be far below the growth of sales and direct costs. When you see distortions in these relationships, it should raise questions about the timing of expense recognition.

Current expenses can be exaggerated by setting up an unusually high reserve or special charge; by writing off acquisition or research costs too quickly; or by speeding up the rate of expense payments to move more expense into the current year. From 1996 through 1998, Sunbeam had created a $35 million reserve, effectively creating current expenses artificially. In 1997 earnings were increased when the reserve was released. So the reserve creation and release were used to equalize profits and create the illusion of steady growth. Both Cisco and Toys "R" Us wrote off expenses and created reserves, duplicating a similar strategy of creating current expenses for use later when revenues began to lag. Similar questionable accounting practices were attributed during the late 1990s to Compaq Computers; U.S. Robotics; and the Walt Disney Company.

Core Earnings as an Analytical Tool

A significant development in fundamental analysis occurred in 2002. That year Standard & Poor's published a paper called "Measures of Corporate Earnings." This paper introduced a new concept: *core earnings*. S&P defined these as earnings from a corporation's principal business or businesses; excluded from core earnings are nonrepetitive items such as capital gains. The purpose—and value—of this calculation is that it provides you with a reliable summary of the core business and, thus, the likely growth potential of a company over the long term. Because the nonrecurring adjustments so often cloud the growth picture, this S&P standard is now seen as having great value in fundamental analysis.

According to S&P's definition of core earnings, you begin with the reported operated results of a corporation, and add to it the following additional items:

- Losses from the sale of assets (capital assets or operating units)
- Merger and acquisition-related charges and costs
- Litigation proceeds received
- Unrealized losses from hedging activities (investment assets)
- Goodwill impairment charges (accounting adjustments for intangible assets)

Furthermore, the following items have to be deducted from reported earnings:

- Gains from the sale of assets (capital assets or operating units)
- Unrealized gains from hedging activities
- Litigation costs and settlements paid
- Pension gains (net of interest expenses)
- Employee stock options granted

The process of identifying noncore items can be complex and time-consuming, often involving the interpretation of complex financial statement footnotes. For this reason most people can get a fair estimate of the adjustments by concentrating on the major areas such as pension gains, capital gains or losses, profit from the sale of operating units, and employee stock options.

Core earnings adjustments can be quite significant in that they distort results from one year to the next, making all fundamental analysis unreliable. It is imperative that all ratios you use and all trends you develop should be based on *operating* profits, also meaning core earnings. So you need to examine the annual reports of a corporation; find the noncore items included and remove them; and find the noncore items excluded and add them back in. By focusing only on the major adjustments, you simplify the task.

Key Point

Identifying *core* earnings is such a sensible idea, it is surprising that it has not come up before. Then again, the problem with the way financial reporting takes place is its widespread inaccuracy.

If you do not want to make your own core earnings analysis of an annual report, you should ensure that your financial advisor or consultant knows how to make those adjustments and is able to provide you with a simplified summary of the core operations. In addition to making the report of a specific company more reliable, this also makes company-to-company comparisons valid.

Generally speaking, you will find that corporations that are well managed will tend to have a lower volume of core earnings adjustments each year. So many noncore transactions result from periodic accounting changes, restructuring, and attempts to manipulate profits from acquisitions and questionable timing. You will also discover that these well-managed corporations also tend to exhibit lower technical volatility, meaning less broad movement up and down in the stock's price. There is a tendency for well-managed corporations to exhibit both fundamental and technically based low volatility. The two aspects of analysis are directly related, and the level of core earnings adjustments is one test of this phenomenon.

A troubling and related attribute of fundamental analysis involves valuation of the corporation itself. Because expense and revenue levels may be distorted significantly, it follows that some balance sheet accounts—notably liabilities—may be equally distorted. In Chapter 3, you were advised that if General Motors were to record its liability for pension payments, the company would be worthless. This is troubling for any stockholder. The realization that a corporation has no tangible value brings into question the very basis on which stocks are selected and held. Many other corporations would be in the same situation if their balance sheets were entirely accurate. The *core net worth* would be an adjusted valuation of corporate net worth based on making realistic adjustments to all asset and liability accounts, a suggestion that many corporations, including some long-standing Blue Chips, do not want to consider.

core net worth

the net worth of a corporation reflecting the accurate and total value of all assets and liabilities, including unrecorded or inaccurately recorded items.

Key Point

The prospect that many large corporations may, in fact, be worthless due to unrecorded liabilities is very troubling. But that does not mean the problem should be ignored. The real fix is to reform accounting standards so that everything—even the bad news—is made completely transparent.

The many problems of unreliable reporting, inaccurate accounting, and overly flexible GAAP rules make fundamental analysis far more complex than many people believe. The accounting industry has not taken a lead role in reforming its inadequate system, so every investor needs to consider alternatives to dependence on audited financial statements. The next chapter offers one solution: using confirmation, an idea introduced within the Dow Theory, to test trends and to determine if companies are providing you with accurate information.

Chapter

Confirmation: The Trend of the Trends

Facts are seldom facts, but what people think are facts, heavily tinged with assumptions.
—Harold Geneen, *Managing*, 1984

Using fundamental analysis, you try to narrow down a field of likely investment candidates. You apply ratios of various types as you will discover in the following three chapters; and you attempt to locate the *best possible* stocks. If you seek long-term growth, high dividends, low price volatility, and strong capitalization, these criteria can narrow your selection down from several thousand potential stocks to a few dozen.

Even when you can only focus on a handful of stocks, you are left with the problem of interpretation. How do you use the data you gather to generate a decision to buy; and once you own stock, how do you know when to sell? The answers begin in the analysis of trends, of course. But when new information comes your way, you must be able to test that information to ensure that you are correct in acting upon it.

This is where the process of confirmation becomes a valuable tool. This involves verification of discovered trends—good or bad—by checking other trends to either justify (confirm) or contradict what the first trend indicated. Using confirmation in this way improves the chances that your decisions will be good decisions.

The Dow Theory and Confirmation

The Dow Theory is the centerpiece of technical analysis. Its principles, developed after Charles Dow's death and applied to a series of indices, include identification of major trends (involving confirmation between separate index movements). The purpose to the Dow Theory is to gauge the conditions of the market as a whole, based on prices within the indices. So in the case of the Dow Jones Industrial Average (DJIA), the market is quantified by price movement in 30 stocks. Because those stocks are so large and represent a large portion of total market capitalization and trading activity, technicians consider the DJIA a reasonable barometer of market conditions and trends.

Key Point

Using well-designed indices is a popular way to judge the current sentiment of the market; but remember, indices tell you virtually nothing about an individual stock.

Today, most market observers follow the DJIA along with price trends in the NASDAQ stock index and the S&P 500. When all of these primary indices are reviewed together (as well as utility and transportation indices and numerous other market indicators), technical analysts develop an opinion about bull and bear trends within the overall market. Those conditions are good for overall analysis; and when technical analysis is reduced to individual stocks, two broad tools are employed.

- *Larger market comparison.* First is the broader market, in other words the indices and the current mood and major trend (bull or bear), especially as that larger trend may or may not affect the price of an individual stock. This *beta* is a method used to compare an individual stock's volatility to the volatility in the market at large. If beta is 1, it means that the stock generally changes price in the same direction as the larger market. The lowest beta, 0, indicates that a stock is unresponsive to larger market movements; and the highest beta, 2, indicates that a stock is highly volatile in comparison to the larger market.

beta

a technical test of a stock's volatility in comparison to the market as a whole. The degree to which a stock's price historically tracks larger market price movement determines its beta.

- *Specific stock price trends.* The technician also judges individual stock price based on charting, trading range, price volatility over various time spans, and breakouts (above resistance or below support levels).

These two technical indicators both serve as a form of confirmation. Under the Dow Theory, overall market trends are confirmed by directional movement in a primary and then in a secondary index. On the individual stock price basis, a chart pattern indicates a change in trend and is believed to anticipate price movements yet to come. The beta of the stock provides the technician a way to confirm that belief. For example, if a stock is highly volatile and a sharp downturn in the market occurs (as measured by the DJIA), does this signal anything of significance in the stock itself? This apparent signal may be confirmed if the stock's price tests the resistance level (at the top of the trading range) two or more times unsuccessfully. This may forecast a sharp downward price movement in the stock in the near future.

This example demonstrates the power of confirmation. An indication based on a change in an index may be confirmed by a chart pattern in the stock. Because both of these imply the same pending change, the technician may be able to make investment decisions about near-term price changes.

A confirmation process has been used in technical analysis for many decades and, often, with success. However, it remains controversial because many technical indicators have not consistently anticipated prices. The Dow Theory acknowledges that short-term price changes are not reliable as firm indicators of coming changes, and confirmation itself is based on changes in two major indices. So it is widely accepted and believed that the chaotic short-term price movements of stocks are not reliable. The market forces are often contradictory and too numerous to be reliable as tools for making immediate decisions.

This brings the discussion to the question of how fundamental analysis may make good use of the confirmation concept. In fact, although associated strongly with technical analysis, confirmation is a reliable and effective tool on the financial side as well.

Key Point

Marketwide trends are useful when reviewed over the long term. But short-term price changes are highly chaotic; making any decisions based on this week's index movement is a mistake.

Using Technical Tools in the Fundamentals

Analysts within the corporation—often called budgetary employees, internal auditors, or corporate accountants—use confirmation continually to test, verify, and quantify their own financial estimates. There may be a widespread belief among nonaccountants that financial analysis is a fairly specific science, but in practice it involves a lot of forecasting and estimating.

A good deal of energy goes into budgets and forecasts, the attempt to anticipate future revenues, costs and expenses, profits, and cash flow. The budgeting process may attempt to look forward as far as five years, while the more practical internal controls tend to last only for 12 months. Budgeting is used to control expense levels as an internal procedure; to set marketing goals and benchmarks as a means for monitoring success in the field; and to anticipate and plan for cash flow in the near future.

The same types of activities can be used by investors as part of a program of fundamental analysis. Any time you develop and follow a trend, you anticipate certain developments to occur. If those developments do not occur or if trends flatten out and turn around, it may indicate a change in the company's financial strength or competitive position. Before acting on the apparent meaning of your trend analysis, it makes sense to attempt to confirm the change in the trend by checking other indicators. This is the essence of confirmation, and its applicability to fundamental analysis may be more important than the way it is used in tracking a stock's price. Confirmation is an essential tool in financial budgeting and control; it serves the same purpose to investors as part of a program of fundamental analysis.

Apparent Bad News Explained through Investigation

You have been tracking revenues and earnings for a particular corporation. The latest quarterly financial statement shows an unexpected 10 percent decline in revenues and a 3 percent drop in earnings. Should you sell? Upon further investigation, you discover that the company recently sold off a major operating segment, which explains the drops. In this situation, further information explained the change, so no further action is warranted.

> ### Key Point
>
> The most apparent answer is not always the final answer. Be sure your data is solid before making investment decisions.

Unexplained Ratios Reveal an Unexpected Negative Trend

A company whose stock you own has had declining sales for the past three years and has also reported net operating losses. However, you believe that the company remains a good long-term hold stock. But you are puzzled. The current ratio (comparison between current assets and current liabilities) has remained steady throughout the period of losses, which does not make sense. When you investigate more, you discover that the company has been issuing long-term bonds and keeping proceeds in cash. This artificially makes working capital appear healthy, but a growing portion of future earnings will have to be used to pay interest on the bonds, meaning less profits for shareholder dividends. With this news—confirming that something did not make sense based on your tracking of ratios—you decide to cut your losses and sell.

> ### Key Point
>
> If something just does not add up, investigate further. You might discover interesting and revealing answers you did not expect to find.

Confirmation Used to Contradict an Apparent Trend

You own a stock in a company whose sales are growing each year at a healthy clip. However, you note that the dollar amount of profits has remained about the same, but the percentage of earnings to revenues has been declining. You investigate further and discover that both costs and expenses have been climbing at a faster rate than revenues, which explains the lack of earnings growth. Should you sell? When you look back over the company's last three annual reports, you realize that a new acquisition occurred, and its operating structure involves higher costs and expense levels. Based on the justification for acquiring the company and upon the stated long-term growth plan, you decide that the apparent problem is transitional—you do not sell.

> ### Key Point
>
> Some seemingly negative trends are not negative at all but the result
> of changes in the mix of business, in other words, potentially good
> trends over the long term.

Discovery of a Trend and Confirmation

You own a stock whose recent price has begun demonstrating far higher
volatility than in the past. This change is troubling because no obvious
reasons have been given. However, when you review the financial history,
you discover an increasing level of nonrecurring profits from sale of assets
and accounting policy changes. Based on the volume of fundamental
volatility, you conclude that the technical (price) volatility is a symptom
of management's decisions over the past few years. At the moment, the
stock is at a high relative to recent activity, and higher than your original
purchase price. You decide to sell now rather than remain at risk for
volatile price changes, and additionally, to the possibility of fundamental
instability in the future.

> ### Key Point
>
> Even though you concentrate on fundamental indicators, you can
> also use the technical (i.e., price) to confirm a decision.

Confirming Both Good News and Bad News

The process of confirmation should be aimed at discovering the truth
about what is going on and to enable you to forecast the relative financial
strength of a corporation in the near future. With this in mind, confirmation may reveal either good news or bad news. Ultimately, a better
quality of information is the key. The more you understand what is occurring and why, the better able you are to make intelligent decisions.

You may employ fundamental ratios for multiple purposes. The
most obvious purpose is to identify strong long-term investments and,
after buying, to spot changing trends. A second purpose of, perhaps,
equal importance, is to flag potentially deceptive or misleading reporting
on the part of the corporation or its auditors.

The numbers reveal everything, ultimately. However, this statement has to be qualified. The numbers reveal everything within the scope of what you are shown. A major flaw in accounting standards is in the fact that so many significant items can be left out—and are left out. You do not get the whole picture. Pension liabilities, contingent liabilities due to pending lawsuits, and long-term lease and purchase commitments are a few examples of potentially major liabilities and, of course, their corresponding expenses. So how do you manage this problem?

To get the full picture, you need to employ the fundamental ratios and follow classic trends that will be explained in coming chapters. You also need to look beyond the financial statements by reading the footnotes and identifying the liabilities that have *not* been listed for you. Full disclosure, in the spirit of transparency, *should* be the standard. It would be a vast improvement if the major impact of items buried in the footnotes were explained in a plain-English attachment to the financial statements. But this information is not provided. You need to become adept at finding information in the footnotes and in determining how significant they are. Specifically, you need to be able to judge how much impact these off-balance sheet liabilities and future expenses are going to have on long-term growth. If you are unwilling or unable to delve into the footnotes, then you need to work with a fundamentally based financial planner or analyst who can do that for you; or to participate in an investment club and split up the analytical duties among many other members. The task is not easy, but it is essential.

Key Point

Sadly, real transparency is lacking in most financial reports. To get an accurate picture, you need to perform your own financial analysis.

Given the complexity of getting the entire financial picture, it makes sense that many investors give up on the fundamentals and try to time their buy and sell decisions based on price movement of the stock. But you can glean a lot of valuable information by following specific trends in your search for better information, even when some items are not disclosed on the statements themselves.

For example, if you track *cash flow* of the corporation, you can identify not only cyclical changes in revenues and earnings, but also watch

cash flow
the trail of funds
moving in and out
of the organiza-
tion, which can be
tracked and
watched as a
means for deter-
mining fiscal
health. Cash flow
management
determines how
effectively an
organization is
able to fund cur-
rent and future
operating de-
mands and
growth.

how corporations plan for their liabilities. If a corporation is in the middle of litigation, reserves may
be set up in the liability section of the balance sheet
with a corresponding expense for litigation settle-
ment costs. In this way, the off-balance sheet items
come to light. Because the reserve would be a current liability, it also impacts working capital and, by
implication, the ratios you use to follow cash flow.

Also keep an eye on long-term debt. Remember, cash flow can be made to look healthy even
when it is not, if the corporation increases its long-
term debt to bolster cash or inventory, or to offset
gradually increasing obligations. These obligations
may not show up on the balance sheet; if long-term
lease contracts (which are not listed as liabilities) require high monthly payments out of working capital,
the normal ratios are not going to explain changes in
cash flow. Ideally, the analysis of working capital compares current assets to
current liabilities; but if the corporation is committed to monthly lease payments not included in current liabilities, then there is a problem.

In your use of fundamental indicators to discover either good news or
bad news, the footnotes are essential. You cannot rely on the traditional,
yet incomplete balance sheet and operating statement, because too much is
left to footnote disclosures only. And it is not all negative. While many important liabilities may be left off (even to the extent of completely eliminating net worth in some cases, such as General Motors), there may also be
positive adjustments. Under the traditional accounting rules, assets have to
be listed at original purchase price minus depreciation. So over time these
assets decline to zero value. But consider what happens when a corporation
owns a large amount of real estate. That real estate can grow substantially
in value over time, even while the balance sheet value has declines each
year. So if you need to judge a company's net worth realistically, it is important to read the footnotes to determine current market value of assets
and not merely accept the values shown on the balance sheet.

It is clear that the accounting rules leave much to be desired, not
only in what is not included on the statements, but also in the way that
complete explanations are not offered. This problem may eventually be
resolved; however, for the nonaccountant investor who needs information
today, the problems of how to use financial information are significant.

Key Point

The accounting industry does not work for the individual investor. It works for those who pay the bills, the corporations reporting transactions—and often, with the strongest motivation to obscure what is going on.

Using the traditional ratios to monitor and test financial strength, profitability, and net worth will ultimately offset even the problems involved with nondisclosure. Even those liabilities left off of the balance sheet eventually find their way into the numbers, so as you track ratios over time, the true and complete picture emerges. Unfortunately, you do not receive much help from the auditing industry, whose emphasis is on verification of the financial data that are included on the financial statements. As a general rule, whenever you see a shift in a trend—whether involving profitability, capital strength, or working capital—look first to the numbers you are provided on the financial statements and then to the footnotes. The answers are there, although they may not be apparent at first.

An exception to this general rule is the case where intentional fraud has occurred, or where the information is carefully hidden in complex off-balance sheet transactions. Many of the cases of corporate misrepresentation and manipulation of the numbers involved this type of activity. If you cannot make sense out of the numbers, there often is a good reason.

For example, a corporation may set up a foreign subsidiary specifically to create tax write-offs. Here is how it works: A subsidiary is established in a country that does not collect income taxes. That subsidiary is funded and then makes a loan to the parent company. The parent company makes interest payments to the subsidiary. Those payments are deductible, so they reduce domestic federal and state taxes; but, no taxes have to be paid for the subsidiary.

This simplified example of how corporations can use international law and the tax rules to manipulate profits is only one of many ways that the numbers are controlled. But the whole transaction is a sham. There is no legitimate lending and borrowing going on and, if this is discovered, the deduction would be disallowed. It is even possible that the corporation and the auditing firm would be in trouble for setting up the sham transaction, and in the case of the auditor, for not red-flagging the obvious false transaction. Throughout the 1990s and through 2003, dozens of big-number lawsuits were filed by stockholders against auditing firms for allowing corporations to artificially inflate earnings; control fundamental volatility by shifting revenues and expenses; and otherwise deceiving investors by allowing corporations to create a false picture of their operating results.

The Problem of Time and Fundamentals

Given the complexity of analyzing financial statements—if only because so much is left off of them—it is important to identify a short list of trends you do want to track. Making decisions to buy, hold, or sell stock has to be made on some initial premise that (1) the indicated financial strength and long-term growth potential are realistic; (2) those trends will continue and, as long as they do, you will remain invested; and (3) the financial reports you receive are, for the most part, complete and accurate.

Key Point
Every investment decision you make is premised on some basic assumptions. While this is necessary, it is also useful to *confirm* those assumptions by checking on some issues beyond the numbers, such as management's integrity.

You need to trust in the integrity of management as a starting point. This may even be considered an intangible but crucial starting point in identifying companies that you would consider owning. The well-known reputation of management, a record of profitability, and the lack of regulatory fines are all positive indicators. However, if there is ongoing controversy about a CEO's practices and integrity, and if investigations are continuous, it may indicate that there remain questionable issues—legal, ethical, and management-oriented.

Beyond the question of whether management is qualified, ethical, and operating within the law, a chronic problem of fundamental analysis needs to be managed: the timing of what you receive and use, and the validity of the decisions you make.

Technicians criticize fundamental analysis because it is based on the past. Financial information you use today may be weeks or even months out of date and the situation is likely to emerge and evolve in unexpected ways. Because of the methodical way that quarterly statements are published, it is difficult to get information that is timely and valid. In comparison, technicians can track a stock's price by the minute, and their decisions are based on how prices change during the trading day.

For anyone who makes investment decisions based on outdated information takes a risk. However, it is also possible to operate on a series of reasonable assumptions. Some examples include:

1. *Similarity between outdated and current PE ratios.* Outdated information does not mean that fundamental analysis is invalid. You can perform numerous comparative analyses to judge whether the status of a company remains the same as it was in the past. The PE ratio is an excellent test of earnings-price status. Because PE compares price (a technical indicator) to earnings (a fundamental indicator), it is an especially interesting and popular trend to follow. If the price has changed substantially, you would also expect PE to change; but the current PE may be based not on the latest final financial statement, but on more recent filings. So tracking PE helps to ensure that the relative value of price and earnings is consistent or, when PE does change significantly, that the relationship has changed. As a guiding principle, if either earnings or price have changed drastically since the last published financial statement, that may serve as a reason to hold off making decisions, at least until more updated indicators become available.

2. *Consistency or improvement in dividend rates.* One of the most valuable fundamental indicators is the dividend payment. It is constantly updated, and for many investors, it serves as one of the more important deciding points. Some investors limit their review to those corporations paying exceptionally high dividends (for example, rates higher than 4 percent). Others limit their field of possible investments to corporations whose dividend has been increased each year for many years. For example, Tootsie Roll, Pfizer, Johnson & Johnson, Heinz, Altria, Procter & Gamble, Colgate-Palmolive, Marsh & McLennan, Eli Lilly, Emerson Electric, PepsiCo, Target, Diebold, Hormel, McGraw-Hill, Chubb, Fuller, 3M, and Gannett are among corporations that have increased their dividend payment every year for more than 30 years.

3. *Similar stock price relative to financial condition.* Even when you limit your analysis to fundamentals, stock price can be a confirming indicator. For example, if today's stock price is approximately the same as it was on the date of the last audited financial statement, it may indicate that nothing has changed drastically. This is especially true if the PE ratio has also remained about the same.

4. *Long-term strength in operating trends.* Tracking revenues and earnings should be a centerpiece in every program of fundamental analysis. When a corporation reports consistent sales growth and net return, it is a reliable long-term indicator. Even if the latest statement is outdated, the long-term trend is reassuring; and by checking recent financial news for the corporation, you can glean updated revenues and earnings numbers, even if these are only indicators. What you want to look for is any unexpected surprises. For long-term, consistent financial reports of a company, you may rely, at least in part, on the low fundamental volatility that characterizes the organization.

5. *Confirmation of annual financial reports via interim filings.* Even when the latest audited financial statement is months out of date, all listed companies file quarterly financial statements with the SEC. These 10-Q filings provide interim details and can be relied upon to provide current information about the corporation's revenues and earnings.

Confirmation to Help Avoid Misreading the Trend

The value of using confirmation is that it helps you to avoid misunderstanding the trends. One example was provided in the previous section. If you are reviewing financial information but the latest audited statement is several months out of date, you may *assume* all remains the same because the stock price is also about the same level. However, to confirm this assumption, also check the PE. If it is also at about the same level, the initial assumption is confirmed. Admittedly, this level of analysis is sparse and far from conclusive; but it does provide a starting point for the belief that there are no earnings surprises afoot.

Key Point
Finding and tracking trends is fairly easy. The real work starts when you take steps to confirm what you see, and when you find ways to make sure you are not misreading what the trend tells you.

It is all too easy to misread the trend. Confirmation requires that you check a secondary indicator, and it is most useful when something does not make sense on its own. For example, a corporation has reported large net losses for the last three years, but its current ratio remains strong. How is this accomplished? A review of long-term liabilities demonstrates an increase in bonds issued, with proceeds left in the form of cash. In this instance the appearance of strong working capital is deceptive because over the long term, the corporation will need to use current earnings to relay its debts. This means lower dividends and profits, affecting equity investment value—especially if the trend to weak operating results continues.

In this case a puzzling and unexplained ratio was investigated. It did not make sense that the working capital analysis would remain consistent when the corporation was also reporting losses. Confirmation achieved with a check of the source of the current ratio (assets and liabilities) provided the answers. The ratio was artificial because of the increase in long-term debt.

You will see similar aberrations on the operating results as well. For example, when a corporation has reported consistent growth in revenues and regular net returns, why is the latest quarter so far below the average? Several possible reasons may contribute to the situation, beyond the obvious possibility that the trend has turned. The condition may be cyclical, and this possibility can be confirmed by reviewing results for the same quarters in previous fiscal years. (In retail industries, you would expect to see a very strong end-of-year volume and relatively weak volume for the first quarter.) Each industry has its own cyclical changes in volume and profits. Another possibility is the sale of a major operating unit, whose contribution of revenues and earnings was significant. It could also be affected by the acquisition of a new company whose mix of business and profitability is vastly different from the parent company, with current quarterly results including a high net loss for the newly acquired company.

Key Point
Why do sales and earnings growth curves slow down or even stop? The answer might not be as obvious as most people believe.

In other words, confirmation is a means for looking beyond the initial assumption. Those initial beliefs are often wrong because other contributing factors are in play. So using core earnings analysis to remove nonrecurring items, restating prior years' results for major changes such as acquisitions or disposals of operating units, and recognition of interim economic and market cycles are among the many possible reasons for sudden surprises. Also look for changes in major ratios that may explain why working capital remains strong even as operating results weaken. If corporations artificially bolster their fundamentals, it will be revealed by applying those confirming tests.

Common Mistakes and How to Avoid Them

Many investors, even those experienced in fundamental analysis, are likely to make errors in assumptions and in reading the trends. These mistakes include the following:

1. *Forgetting that trends tend to level out over time.* Any long-term statistical study involves an evening out of the trend. No trend line is going to continue indefinitely, at the established rate, or without change. It is unrealistic, for example, to expect a corporation to report 25 percent increases in revenues each and every year, just because they have done so for the past three years. This observation is especially true in the case of growth. A 25 percent increase in sales will be based on the previous year's levels. So by necessity, the dollar amount needs to be greater each year. Because all markets are finite, it is impossible to sustain a high growth rate forever. Keep this in mind as you observe trends beginning to flatten out over time. It is not necessarily a negative sign, and as long as other capital and profitability ratios remain strong, leveling out of one trend is not always a negative sign.

2. *Misinterpreting a short-term or nonrepetitive matter as a trend.* One of the more difficult aspects to analysis is the interpretation of

data. A common mistake is to take a solitary signal and assume it represents a new trend. Confirmation requires not only independent proof supporting an apparent trend, but time as well. In order for a change to become a trend, it has to last for some period of time without reversal. Some short-term changes or nonrepetitive spikes in growth look like trends, but they are only short-term aberrations.

3. *Looking in the wrong area for confirmation.* Finding valid confirmation requires some experience. When seeking confirmation from other trends or applying other ratios, make sure they do confirm the original indicator. It makes sense to confirm an apparent trend in working capital by also reviewing long-term debt and capitalization; it would make no sense to draw conclusions about working capital based on trends in fixed asset depreciation. And the strong relationship between sales, costs, expenses, and profits points the way to important trends and the use of valuable ratios; but you cannot judge profitability by isolating a review to changes in accounts receivable or inventory levels alone. While those current account levels will certainly change during periods of expansion in revenues, they are not going to tell the whole story.

4. *Misreading a confirmation signal.* Even upon finding valid data, you still must be able to read it well. For example, when you see accounts receivable balances growing, that alone is not proof that the company is expanding its revenues and earnings effectively. A more detailed analysis may reveal that unpaid balances are remaining on the book longer now than in previous quarters, and bad debts are on the rise. These negative trends point to internal control problems, so that even with increased revenues being generated, the net return will ultimately suffer if the control problem is not fixed. In other words, a trend may mean one thing in a set of circumstances and another thing when those circumstances change. For example, you may limit your review of operating results to revenues. An impressive expansion in volume of sales is a promising sign, but not if net profits are declining. That is a danger signal, a sign that in the period of expansion, management has relaxed its internal controls. It is not unusual for profits to decline during times when revenues are on the rise.

5. *Giving too much credence to technical (thus, short-term) indicators.* Every investor who follows the fundamentals is susceptible to temptation. Following price trends is easy; the information is updated every day and it is easy to find. So it often occurs that even with a lot of fundamental groundwork, decisions end up being made based on price movement and other technical indicators. This is why profit taking is so common, and why so many fundamental investors end up making mistakes (like buying high and selling low instead of the other way around). If you stay with long-term fundamental indicators as a guiding force, you will be more confident in ignoring short-term price volatility.

6. *Overlooking obvious danger signals, such as chronic operating losses.* Everyone has heard the theme that "reporting a net loss is all right." There is no justification for this belief. A loss is just that, a failed year. It is a reduction of net worth and a *problem* for every investor. No one really wants to put money behind a company that does not report a profit. Amazingly, many companies that have never reported a profit are able to raise capital, based on hype and the willing support of investment bankers. A look back to the dot.com days proves the point. But remember, a company without any history of profits has, essentially, no fundamentals to study. So how do you make any judgment about such a company? The lack of profit history is one of the more glaring examples of an obvious danger signal. Others may include a loss of leadership within an industry; pending and ongoing litigation; big-scale labor disputes; regulatory problems, such as corporate officers being accused of mail fraud and, more than anything else, extreme volatility in the numbers. Do not forget that well-managed companies experience volatility now and then, but not every year. High fundamental volatility, large-scale core earnings adjustments, and technical volatility are all signs of uncertain management or an out-of-control internal environment.

In the next chapter, you will begin to see a methodical explanation of actual ratios, which become the building block of long-term trends. Balance sheet ratios are often overlooked because some people believe the operating ratios are more interesting and revealing. As you will see, balance sheet analysis tells just as much about profitability as operating ratios—and in certain cases they are even more revealing.

Balance Sheet Ratios
Making the Analysis

The greater the wealth, the thicker will be the dirt. This indubitably describes a tendency of our time.
—John Kenneth Galbraith, *The Affluent Society*, 1958

nyone who approaches financial statements for the first time is likely to be overwhelmed by the volume of numbers, values, footnotes, and complexity of the entire matter. For this reason, it makes sense to break down the various types of ratios you use to build trends, by the type of financial statement involved.

A ratio is an expression of financial values, in a greatly reduced form. This makes it easier to comprehend the significance of the relationships between values. So 3 to 1 is more readily comprehended than $635,418,438 to $211,806,146. Ratios may be expressed in the format shown above, *x* to *y*. Some ratios are expressed in percentage form or as a single numerical value. For example, net return (earnings divided by revenues) is usually expressed as a percentage; and the PE ratio is usually expressed as a single value. When a stock's price is $38 per share and earnings per share are $1.13, the PE is 34 (38 ÷ 1.13). Another expression is by "number of times" an event occurs. Any ratio involving turnover (explained later in this chapter) is summarized as the number of times an event occurs per year.

Key Point

Ratios are expressed in a number of formats, depending on the type of shorthand financial summary they are designed to express.

Ratios exist and are expressed in these various formats, and they serve as the building blocks of trends. In order to track several fundamental trends, you need to be able to understand the significance of a broad range of ratios. These include values in at least three different formats: balance sheet ratios, income statement ratios, and ratios that combine fundamental and technical information. Examples include PE, dividend yield, and other ratios comparing a stock's price to fundamental results. In this chapter, you will find a range of *balance sheet ratios*. These involve comparisons between two related account balances found on a company's balance sheet.

balance sheet ratios
those ratios comparing account balances found on a corporation's balance sheet (1) at the end of a period or (2) between years or quarters.

Balance sheet ratios are normally associated with tests performed on the same date. The balance sheet summarizes the values of assets, liabilities, and net worth as of the close of a quarter or fiscal year; so most balance sheet ratios involve testing and analyzing the values as of the same date. However, one area of great interest to fundamental analysts is following trends in individual accounts from period to period. So data may be analyzed for a single account or combination of accounts from year to year. These may include the net difference between current assets minus current liabilities; long-term debt; net worth; net long-term assets; and any other account or accounts that reveal something of value. In the next chapter, you will see that year-to-year tracking has many applications in operating results; but following relationships within the balance sheet is also instructive.

To review, the balance sheet contains three major sections and, within each section, a series of subdivisions:

Assets

Current assets (cash and items convertible to cash within 12 months)

Long-term assets (capital investments net of accumulated depreciation)

Other assets (intangible, prepaid, and deferred assets)

Liabilities

Current liabilities (obligations payable within the next 12 months)

Long-term liabilities (obligations payable beyond the next 12 months)

Deferred credits

Net Worth (also called Shareholders' Equity)

Capital stock outstanding

Retained earnings

Other net worth accounts and adjustments

Current Assets and Liabilities

To begin an analysis of balance sheet ratios, the first step is to ensure that the meanings of "current" assets and liabilities are understood fully. The distinction between current and long-term is crucial for defining the financial health of an organization.

Working capital, or the net difference between the value of current assets and current liabilities, is a defining feature of the corporate balance sheet. Short-term liquidity—the availability of cash to fund ongoing operations—is an essential starting point in fundamental analysis, and this cornerstone involves a series of tests relating to how current assets and liabilities change over time—seasonally, during periods of growth, and over the long term.

Key Point
A "current" asset is supposed to be available in the form of cash within 12 months—specifically to pay "current" liabilities, which are due within 12 months.

Current assets include a grouping of accounts that are considered "liquid." The most liquid is cash (balances in various bank accounts); the other current assets are convertible to cash form within one year. These include accounts and notes receivable (amounts due from customers, net of a reserve for bad debts); inventory of goods for sale, usually reported at original cost *or* at current market value; and marketable securities (liquid investments owned by the company, such as stocks, bonds, or money market accounts).

Current liabilities include all debts the company is obligated to pay within the next 12 months. This would include current accounts payable; taxes payable (income tax and payroll taxes, for example); dividends payable to shareholders; and 12 months' payments due on all notes, mortgages and contracts.

The current nature of these asset and liability sections interact with one another directly. If a large sum of cash is paid out to reduce current liabilities, the ratios improve but the company will be short of cash. In the next section, you will see how this works, and why it sometimes makes sense for a corporation to manage the relationship between its current accounts. Yet there is more to it than just how and when cash is spent. Control over current levels of accounts receivable and inventory are also crucial measurements of how well a corporation is managing its accounts.

During periods of tremendous growth, there is a tendency for both accounts receivable and inventory levels to rise. Receivable balances go up because more customers are involved with growth, so more accounts are paid on time rather than in cash. As the volume of revenues grows, it also becomes necessary for the company to stock up inventory to ensure that goods are available for timely delivery.

Problems often arise during periods of growth because corporations do not control receivable and inventory trends. As a consequence, they begin having cash flow problems, meaning there is not enough money available to pay current obligations, such as payroll and taxes, vendor statements, and overhead. Ironically, it is growth itself that poses the greatest threat to cash flow health. If a corporation allows its balances in accounts receivable or inventory to outpace the rate of increase in revenues and earnings, trouble may follow. So as you test the current accounts and their relationships, look for trends in working capital, including trends in accounts receivable and inventory balances.

current ratio
a test of working capital, computed by dividing current assets by current liabilities. The result is expressed in the form of *x* to *y* and the general standard for an acceptable current ratio level is 2 to 1 or better.

Working Capital Tests

The first and best-known working capital test is the *current ratio*—a comparison between current assets and current liabilities. To compute, divide current assets by current liabilities:

$$CA \div CL$$

> ### Key Point
>
> The current ratio is one of the most important tests of working capi-
> tal. Remember, it is only one of several tests you need to perform. No
> single ratio is ever conclusive by itself.

For example, you are studying the balance sheet of three corporations. The following levels of current assets and liabilities are reported for
the latest dates:

Corporation	Current Assets	Current Liabilities
A	$416,311,290	$206,113,915
B	111,042,698	78,418,433
C	316,003,635	105,623,001

The current ratios for these three examples are:

A = 2.0 to 1

B = 1.4 to 1

C = 3.0 to 1

While the 2 to 1 standard is easily applied in numerous situations,
the actual applicability of this standard should vary by industry,
longevity of the company, position in its industry, and overall capital
strength. Additionally, the makeup of the operating statement dictates
the relevance of the current ratio.

A corporation may also rearrange its obligations to improve its current ratio. For example, the second corporation in the example above
showed $111,042,698 in current assets and $78,418,433 in current liabilities, resulting in a 1.4 to 1 current ratio. Had the corporation paid off
$45,000 in current liabilities, its resulting numbers would have shown
$66,042,698 in current assets and $33,418,433 in current liabilities, or a
current ratio of 2.0 to 1 (rounded). So it is possible for corporations to
time payment of current liabilities to control the level of the current ratio, at least to a degree.

> ### Key Point
>
> Be aware that by timing payment of current liabilities, it is quite easy for a corporation to make a current ratio appear more positive than it really is.

The ratio is normally useful when tracking the numbers within one company, and for spotting developing trends. It is less applicable for comparisons between two different companies. For example, if you compare IBM (http://www.ibm.com) to Microsoft (http://www.microsoft.com), the situation in each corporation's overall financial status is quite different. In fact, while a casual observer may classify both of these corporations as belonging within a general "computer" industry, it is not completely accurate. IBM's primary source of revenues is hardware, whereas Microsoft makes most of its sales with software. As a result, IBM's gross profit is far lower, percentage-wise, than Microsoft's, which is quite high. IBM depends on maintaining a high inventory of tangible materials, but Microsoft stocks only its mass-produced software products.

Microsoft also carries virtually no long-term debt on its balance sheet, further complicating a comparison. Because these corporations are structured so differently, it would not be valid to make a company-to-company comparison. However, it may be instructive to compare the trend in the current ratio for each company over many years. As of December 31, 2004, IBM reported total assets and liabilities (in millions of dollars) as:

	Assets	*Liabilities*
Totals	$109,183	$79,436
Current	46,970	39,398
Current ratio		1.2 to 1

Microsoft's fiscal year ended on June 30, and its 2004 financial statement showed:

	Assets	*Liabilities*
Totals	$92,389	$17,564
Current	70,566	14,969
Current ratio		4.7 to 1

This comparison demonstrates the complexity of the current ratio. First, it would seem logical that the current ratio is less important in the case of Microsoft because it does not have to deal in hardware or carry large tangible inventory. Second, the company has almost no long-term debt, so cash flow is far less of an issue. In comparison, IBM has a lot of long-term debt and has to keep inventory on hand; but its financial strength and history are solid. Even so, IBM's current ratio is only 1.2 to 1. Does this mean IBM is a weak company, financially speaking? No; in fact, because these corporations are so different, the comparison would not be valid. You may prefer to track IBM's current asset history over time as well as other ratios.

Key Point

A ratio is of only limited value by itself. To judge the significance of a ratio, it has to be reviewed as it evolves, over time.

---

acid test
a ratio similar to the current ratio, but excluding inventory. The general standard for an "acceptable" acid test is 1 to 1 between current assets (without inventory) and current liabilities. Also called *quick assets ratio*.

This raises a second important test, known as the *quick assets ratio*, also called the *acid test*. This is identical to the current ratio with the exception that inventory is excluded. For companies with exceptionally high inventory, the acid test may be a more accurate indicator to track, because the high inventory may distort the true working capital picture. Returning to the example of IBM and Microsoft, we discover the following:

	Assets	*Inventory*	*Net*	*Liabilities*
Current assets	$46,970	$3,316	$43,654	$39,398
Acid test				1.1 to 1

Microsoft's fiscal year ended on June 30, and its 2004 financial statement showed:

	Assets	*Inventory*	*Net*	*Liabilities*
Current assets	$92,389	$421	$91,968	$17,564
Acid test				5.2 to 1

quick assets ratio

a variation of the current ratio, also called the *acid test*. The general standard for an acceptable quick assets ratio is 1 to 1 between current assets (without inventory) and current liabilities.

inventory turnover

a test of management's efficiency in keeping inventory levels at the right general range. High turnover indicates that inadequate supplies are held, and a trend toward lower rates of turnover indicates poor use of working capital or stocking of slow-moving goods.

The general standard for an acceptable acid test is 1 to 1. Under this standard, IBM reports at an acceptable level, given this general rule. However, just as the current ratio should be limited to analysis from year to year within a single corporation, the acid test should not be applied between dissimilar companies or between companies and the general 1 to 1 standard.

Another area of interest in analyzing working capital is *inventory turnover*, the number of times, on average, that inventory is replace during the year. In practice, inventory is not entirely sold off and replaced, but the averages are significant. The number of turns indicates how efficiently a company manages its inventory levels. A high number of turns may indicate that the company is not maintaining adequate inventory levels for its revenues levels. Yet if the year-to-year turnover rate begins to decline, that could demonstrate that the company is overinvested in inventory, or that it is holding obsolete or slow-moving stock.

Calculation of turnover can be achieved in several ways. Some analysts prefer using revenues in the calculation; but this is not reliable, as it compares inventory at cost to revenues at marked-up levels; if the mix of business varies, the turnover will not be accurate. A more reliable method is to compare inventory to the cost of sales. The formula is to divide cost of sales (*COS*) by *average* inventory (*I*) at cost:

$$COS \div I$$

To find average inventory, the easiest solution is to use beginning and ending inventory levels, divided by two. However, in cases where inventory levels fluctuate significantly throughout the year, it would be more realistic to use quarter-ending inventory levels, which are available on each corporation's 10-Q filed with the SEC. Variation in inventory levels may occur due to cyclical changes throughout the year. For example, a retail corporation whose fiscal year ends December 31 may report beginning and ending inventory levels that are quite low; but at peak periods throughout the year, such as the end of the third quarter, inventory may have been substantially higher.

Key Point

In determining the *average* of anything, make sure you include enough dates so that your average is truly representative of the entire year. This is especially important for companies that go through market cycles.

A final working capital test involves analysis of accounts receivable balances and trends. Testing relative levels of accounts receivable is revealing, notably during times of revenue expansion. When a company's revenues grow rapidly, there may be a tendency to allow three negative trends to develop:

1. *Increased bad debts.* It may be entirely reasonable for a corporation to experience a higher dollar value of bad debts during times of expansion. The negative trend occurs when the rate of growth in bad debts exceeds the rate of growth in earnings.

2. *Longer time required to collect outstanding balances.* A tendency during expansion periods is to relax internal collection controls. It has been accurately observed that when such efforts are relaxed, more accounts become uncollectible. So as the average time bills remain outstanding and unpaid grows, you may also expect to see growth in bad debts.

3. *Accounts receivable expansion outpacing revenue expansion.* As a matter of tracking cash flow, it makes sense to allow the accounts receivable asset to expand somewhat, but not to exceed the cash flow generated from new revenues. It is not enough to track receivables and revenues; you also need to be aware of how the net earnings affect cash flow. The corporation has to pay its costs and expenses, so the valid comparison for accounts receivable expansion should be net profits. If the net dollar amount of increase in receivables is greater than the reported net profit, there may be

problems. This is complicated when only a portion of revenues occur on account and the rest in cash; it is also complicated by the fact that accounts payable may also be growing during periods of expansion.

The comparisons you make between accounts receivable and revenues or earnings should be performed over a number of periods. Otherwise, the trend you develop may be distorted by seasonal variations. This is especially true in industries such as retail, where distinct variations occur during the year.

The common practice is to review receivables and revenues. While this may not reveal the real impact on cash flow, it does provide a trend worth following. Remember, though, that the trend is separate from the actual working capital impact. Based on the mix of revenues between credit and cash, the degree of net earnings, and corresponding growth in other balance sheet accounts (inventory as well as current liabilities, for example), the accounts receivable trends and the working capital outcomes will not always be the same.

Worthwhile ratios to track include:

1. *A simple percentage comparison between accounts receivable balances at the end of a period and total revenues during the period.* Though this trend can be revealing, especially when the trend is negative, it may not be completely accurate to use *all* revenues in the calculation—and it can, in fact, hide a negative trend. It would be more accurate to use only those revenues made on credit. However, without gaining additional information from the corporation, this may be difficult to locate on the typical annual or quarterly statement.

   Here is a solution: If the corporation has reported revenues in different lines of business, credit sales might be more typical for one line than for another. In such instances, isolate your comparison between the total accounts receivable asset and the revenues for the one line of business. Remembering that the ratio will not be entirely accurate, it may reveal an overall trend and provide you with information. At the very least, you may then follow up with contact within the corporation.

2. *Levels of bad debt reserves as a percentage of accounts receivable.* As revenues expand, it is likely that receivables will follow. But to

accurately judge the effectiveness of internal controls, how can you determine whether expansion is reasonable? In a well-managed corporate environment, a reserve for bad debts is set up in the current assets section, as a reduction of accounts receivable—and this negative asset should remain at approximately the same relative level even when revenues and receivables are expanding. When you see the percentage increasing, it indicates that the company is not controlling collections as effectively as it did in the past.

3. *Average time required to collect outstanding accounts.* Another trend that reveals a lot is the average time required to collect money from customers. As the time receivables are outstanding grows, it becomes likely that the company will also experience higher bad debts. In some industries such as financial companies, this type of information is readily available. In some other industries, it might not be as easy to find. So as a practical matter, be aware that you might not find direct evidence of changes in internal policies. Nevertheless, you can draw reasonable conclusions about these accounts by observing rapid expansion of accounts receivable and higher bad debt reserves. The average time works as a confirming indicator, but it is not always easy to find on the annual or quarterly reports, or in the footnotes.

Capitalization: Debt and Equity

The balance sheet provides a wealth of information beyond a corporation's control and management of working capital. As crucial as working capital is to long-term health, there is one other very critical test: *capitalization*.

> **capitalization**
> (1) the equity value of a company, also known as *market capitalization* or *market cap*; it is computed by multiplying total issued shares of common stock by the current price per share; (2) the total debt and equity of a corporation; the combination of net worth and long-term debt.

Key Point

Tracking capitalization is not complex or esoteric. It may reveal far more about cash flow and internal controls than the current ratio.

The concept of capitalization contains two distinct and very different meanings. First is *market*

market capitalization

the market value of all common stock issued and outstanding, computed by multiplying total common shares by the current market price per share.

issued shares

common stock of a listed corporation available for public trading, including closely held shares owned by directors, officers, and founding family members, and the value of shares that may be issued in the future to honor outstanding stock options.

equity

the value of ownership; in a listed corporation, equity consists of all classes of stock plus retained earnings. Equity investors are compensated by way of dividends and long-term capital gains.

capitalization, which is the overall dollar value of common stock's *issued shares*. Information about total shares is found in the balance sheet and its footnotes. If the value of market cap is not provided directly as of the date of the financial statements, it is easily calculated. Simply multiply the number of issued common stock shares by the market price per share. Because both numbers of shares and market price may change over time, market cap is not a stationary number. As a means for comparing overall market value of a company, you may think of market cap as the actual value of common stock. This information is very significant for all stocks included in indices; the larger the market cap, the greater the company's influence on the index. Market cap is also useful for comparisons between corporations within the same industry or for use in calculating various kinds of returns (e.g., return on earnings or investment).

The second definition of capitalization refers to quite a different matter, the distinction and trend between equity and debt. When a corporation's overall capitalization is discussed, it includes two sources. First is *equity*, or ownership, which is represented by the value of the net worth section of the balance sheet (all shares of stock plus retained earnings and adjustments). Second is *debt*, which is represented by long-term liabilities consisting of both *long-term notes payable* and *bonds*. Together, equity and long-term debt comprise the capitalization or the source of money that funds growth and ongoing operations.

The analysis of capitalization and tracking changes between equity and debt is crucial, not only to working capital health, but also as a measurement of planning and cash control. The debt ratio, often also called the *debt-equity ratio*, tracks debt as a total of capitalization. Increases in the percentage of debt are considered negative. As debt grows over time, future dividend payments to stock-holders are likely to be replaced by ever-growing interest to debtors, as well as further cash flow strain when bonds and other long-term debts become due.

> ### Key Point
>
> Watching how companies manage long-term debt provides you valuable information about long-term value, such as the degree of earnings that will be available to pay future dividends to stockholders . . . or interest to bondholders.

The formula is straightforward. Add up total capitalization (C) (long-term debt and shareholders' equity); and then divide long-term debt (D) by the total, with the answer expressed as a percentage (R, or ratio):

$$D \div C = R$$

A potential danger to long-term growth is found in cases where debt capitalization grows over time. During periods when revenues and earnings are down, there may be a tendency for corporate management to fund operations by increasing long-term debt rather than cutting expenses and consolidating operations. This decision has negative long-term ramifications and, without the debt ratio, it may be invisible. For example, if you judge working capital with the current ratio alone, you might never even notice that equity capitalization is being replaced with long-term debt. As mounting net losses continue and equity declines, the corporation may continue to fund its operations and to bolster working capital by accumulating more and more debt.

debt
the value of liabilities of a corporation; to an investor, the value of bonds owned. Bond investors receive compensation by way of interest, as well as discounted value of the bond based on interest rates paid versus current market rates.

long-term notes payable
debts of a corporation that are payable beyond the next 12 months, including intermediate-term loans, mortgages, and long-term obligations.

bonds
for corporations, long-term debts payable with interest to debt investors; for investors, an alternative form of investment including a promise for repayment of principal as well as periodic payments of a stated and fixed rate of interest.

debt-equity ratio

alternate name for the debt ratio; a ratio demonstrating relationships between debt and equity capitalization.

For example, an initial review of Motorola's balance sheet (http://www.motorola.com) over a six-year period reveals some interesting outcomes (see Table 7.1).

These results appear quite promising, as long as the working capital analysis is limited to the current ratio. In fact, it appears that matters have improved significantly. But there is a puzzle. Through 2002, Motorola reported substantial net losses; so how could working capital improve while the company was losing money? In fact, a review of the debt ratio answers this question. During the same period, the debt ratio changed as well (see Table 7.2).

TABLE 7.1 Motorola's Balance Sheet, 1999–2005 (in millions)

Current Year	Current Assets	Current Liabilities	Ratio
1999	$17,585	$12,906	1.4 to 1
2000	19,885	16,257	1.2 to 1
2001	17,149	9,698	1.8 to 1
2002	17,134	9,810	1.7 to 1
2003	7,856	9,381	1.9 to 1
2004	21,115	10,606	2.0 to 1
2005 (6 mos.)	23,216	10,674	2.2 to 1

TABLE 7.2 Motorola's Debt Ratio, 1999–2005 (in millions)

Year	Long-Term Debt	Total Equity	Total Capitalization	Debt Ratio
1999	$3,089	$18,693	$21,782	14.1%
2000	4,293	18,612	22,905	18.7
2001	8,372	13,691	22,063	37.9
2002	7,189	11,239	18,428	39.0
2003	9,976	12,689	22,665	44.0
2004	6,985	13,331	20,316	34.4
2005 (6 mos.)	6,944	14,608	21,552	47.5

This changes the picture considerably. Long-term debt doubled through the period, while equity declined by $4 billion. Total capitalization was approximately the same by mid-2005 as it has been at the end of 1999; but the debt ratio increased from 14.1 percent of the total to nearly *half*, at 47.5 percent.

So the appearance that working capital remained healthy—as measured by the current ratio—is deceptive. You also have to consider that shareholders in this company have to repay the long-term debt that was accumulated at the expense of equity capitalization. In a very real sense, the declining availability of future working capital—brought about by ever-growing long-term debt—may mean lower future dividends. For any stockholders who consider dividend trends an important aspect of valuation, the problem of growing long-term debt may be more important than earnings over the long term.

Key Point

A seemingly unimportant shift in long-term liabilities can, in fact, mask a chronic problem in maintenance of working capital—and create worse working capital problems for many years to come. Ultimately, levels of debt capitalization may define future valuation as much as profits.

The previous example demonstrates the complexity of fundamental analysis. If you limit your review to only one indicator, you have no way to ensure that the results are reliable. In this case, it is perplexing that the current ratio remained strong even while the company reported large net losses. The explanation was found in the replacement of equity with debt, a problem that will plague working capital and cash flow for many years to come.

Ratios between Balance Sheet Periods

Most discussions of balance sheet ratios are limited to the comparison of accounts on the same statement. But equally important are the *trends* that develop over time. Comparing accounts from year to year and tracking trends as they develop—as in the Motorola example—reveal what is really occurring. You cannot isolate a single report and conclusively decide whether the company represents a sound long-term investment, without also looking at the trend itself.

Key Point
Valuable information can be gleaned from a single balance sheet; but it is put in context by seeing how those trends develop over a period of years.

Tracking balance sheet ratios—especially the current ratio, quick assets ratio, and debt ratio—are meaningful measurements of working capital. No single statement can reveal all you need to know; it is important to see where those relationships have been to fully appreciate where they may be headed. What the overall valuation means to you as a potential stockholder has to be determined by a time-specific series of trend observations. Just as you would not judge a stock's market value by looking only at one day's closing price, you cannot make sound judgments about the fundamentals without identifying the trend itself.

This is complicated by restatements. If changes cause a company to change previously reported values on its balance sheet, a long-standing trend may have to be revised completely; and your opinion about a company may also change as a result. The restatement is not always caused by changes in accounting policies or by regulatory action. A common reason restatements are necessary is the purchase of a new company, or the sale of an operating unit.

When corporations acquire new subsidiaries, previous results have to be restated so that the consolidated revenues and earnings reflect the overall results. It may be practical to make reviews of some types by operating segments; but on a practical level this does not reveal all that you need to know. Most corporations do not make clear distinctions between operating segments all the way to the earnings line. Instead, they tend to include all expenses as a single item. You may review revenues and gross profit by operating segments; for any long-term trend analysis involving operating results, however, you will need to revise trends for restatements. This also affects balance sheet valuation. Once a new subsidiary is acquired, the values of accounts receivable and inventory (as well as current liabilities) are also likely to change, not only due to new dollar values, but also because the definition of "reasonable" may change as well given the new mix of business. A corporation, with little or no inventory, may acquire a subsidiary with substantial levels of inventory. That will certainly affect current ratio as well as any working capital analysis such as the relationship between current ratio and quick assets ratio.

When a corporation sells off one of its units, restatements are also necessary and for the same reasons. The loss of ongoing revenues and earnings is accompanied by changes in inventory, accounts receivable, and current liabilities. The whole relationship between past ratios and current ones is going to change, perhaps making the existing trend obsolete. For example, if a company receives a large sum of cash upon completing the sale, its current assets are likely to increase dramatically, so that any trend analysis of working capital will be temporarily distorted. Such changes cannot be used reliably to continue an analysis based on presale values and account relationships.

Off-Balance Sheet Liabilities

A very troubling final observation about balance sheet ratios concerns off-balance sheet liabilities. Most of the trends you develop and track will be affected by obligations that do not show up.

Among the many tricks used by executives in those corporations caught deceiving stockholders in the past, was one in which off-balance sheet liabilities were carried, at times in the billions of dollars. As a consequence, the value of the company and its stock could be vastly inflated. When the balance sheet leaves out important liabilities, it also affects working capital ratios as well as any study of capitalization.

Key Point

One method for judging a corporation is to compare transparency, a company's willingness to disclose everything. Does your company explain off-balance sheet liabilities and provide adjusted ratios for you?

For example, if a corporation has entered into a long-term lease obligation, both current and long-term liabilities are actually much greater than they appear on the balance sheet. You need to go through the notes to the financial statement to discover these very real, but undisclosed liabilities. The footnotes invariably exist; but their significance may not be obvious to the nonaccountant or to the novice investor.

The lack of disclosure may easily distort the true picture, just as increases in long-term debt may distort a seemingly positive trend in the current ratio. The solution is to develop an ability to understand footnotes, and to adjust your trend analysis so that your trends and ratios are complete and realistic. Working through an investment club makes this task easier; using the services of a financial planner who understands the fundamentals is also worth considering.

Even if you perform your own tests, it is not too difficult to develop a series of balance sheet ratios that reveal useful information. Even if liabilities are not included on the financial statement, you can use the information you do have in combination with income statement ratios to gain a fair idea of the company's fiscal health. In the best-managed companies, footnotes are clearly expressed and important ratios may even be calculated for you based on inclusion of items not on the balance sheet. The common problem is an inadequate and antiquated set of accounting rules and the lack of reform, combined with a widespread attitude among corporate executives and auditors that investors don't care about fundamental ratios. However, in reality investors not only care about getting more accurate information; many are frustrated and distrustful of the audited statement and of the complexities of financial reporting. There are solutions, but most investors need to do their own work to find out what is taking place beyond the disclosures on the balance sheet.

The next chapter moves analysis beyond the balance sheet, to the income statement. The ratios and trends you follow on this statement focus on profits and the potential for growth in future earnings.

Chapter

Income Statement Ratios
Tracking the Profits

The easiest job I have ever tackled in this world is that of making money. It is, in fact, almost as easy as losing it. Almost, but not quite.
—H. L. Mencken, *Baltimore Evening Sun*, 1922

The income statement is a summary of revenues, direct costs, expenses, and profits for a specified period of time such as a month, quarter, or fiscal year. The ending date of this period corresponds to the fixed date of the balance sheet. An income statement may cover the period of January 1 through December 31; and the balance sheet published at the same time reports balances of assets, liabilities, and net worth accounts on December 31.

The most popular types of fundamental analysis involve *income statement ratios* because most analysts—both fundamental and technical— recognize the essential role of profits in the valuation of stocks. Even those who only track a stock's price and who have no interest in the financial statements acknowledge that earnings announcements immediately affect stock prices.

This chapter describes and provides examples of such ratios and shows how they reveal specific trends concerning future growth, the value of stock as a potential investment, and the position of a corporation within its own industry.

income statement ratios
tests of financial trends and status based on comparisons between accounts found on the income statement, or outcomes found on income statements and tracked over a period of time.

margin

a gap, remainder, or space between groupings of accounts on the income statement, usually expressed as a percentage; at times interchangeable with "return" and "yield." Typically, analysts study gross margin, operating margin, and pretax margin.

return

the profit remaining when costs and expenses are deducted from revenues; the percentage of profits on original amount invested; or the percentage of profits to equity in a corporation—various types of calculations, usually expressed as a percentage, in analysis of the income statement.

yield

the return, profit, and percentage gained. The term is used on the income statement to compare profits to revenues, amount invested, or equity; or to compare dividends to the current stock price.

Some of the language used in income statement analysis is confusing. You will hear discussions and descriptions of *margin, return,* and *yield.* While these terms have some distinctions, they are often used interchangeably in regard to the income statement. A margin is a remainder, gap, or space between various sections of the statement. For example, the *gross margin* is usually expressed as a percentage, based on the gross profit (revenues minus direct costs) divided by revenues.

A return, like a margin, is expressed as a percentage and the word is often used to mean the same thing as margin. Some ratios, however, such as net return, are popularly used to describe profits to revenues. Return also has broader applications beyond the income statement. For example, *return on equity* is another ratio that compares profits to dollar amounts beyond the income statement.

Yield is distinguished from margin and return because it often is an investment-based calculation rather than one limited to the income statement. "Net yield" is often used as an alternate description of what is more commonly known as *net return.* Yet it is more common to compare a financial value to stock price. For example, the dividend payment during a complete year, divided by the current stock's market value, is called *current yield.*

Key Point

Yield, margin, and return are often used interchangeably. They all mean approximately the same thing and are calculations of either dollar value or percentage of profitability.

In judging profits, there are three distinct types of profits to track. Most investors are aware of net profit, also called earnings and often expressed as earnings per share (EPS). This is often described as the *bottom line* and for good reason: It is the last number on the income statement. However, investors need to ensure that when comparing the "net" from one period to another or between companies, they are using the same values. You need to also be aware of the distinctions between *operating profit* and *pretax profit*.

Operating profit is the profit from revenues minus costs and expenses, but excluding nonoperating income or expense. The pretax profit includes *all* sources of income, costs, and expenses including capital gains, interest, and exchange gains or losses, but without including liabilities for income taxes. The complete income statement, including these various profit/return levels, is summarized in Figure 8.1.

How to Spot the Key Trends

The income statement provides you with a wealth of important information about the company; its growth; and its financial strength. The range of analysis performed from information on income statement includes not only the current outcomes and comparisons, but also comparisons between the current results and past results. The trends are all-important; and you recognize those trends by observing how they evolve over time.

gross margin
the percentage of gross profit to revenues on the income statement.

return on equity
a ratio comparing profits before interest and taxes (operating profit) to a corporation's net worth.

net return
the return on sales, usually expressed as a percentage. Earnings are divided by revenues to determine the net return.

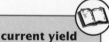

current yield
the percentage return investors earn from dividends paid by a corporation. To calculate, divide the full year's dividend payment by the current stock price. As the stock price falls, current yield rises; and as the stock price rises, current yield declines.

> **Key Point**
>
> Looking at a single income statement reveals some information; but the whole picture emerges only when you look at the numbers over a longer period of time, from one income statement to another.

To find long-term trend information, whether for stocks you own or for those you are thinking of buying, check the "Investor Relations" link on the corporate website. Most companies include links to several years' annual reports, which also contain

Dollar Value	Percentages or Margins of Return
Revenues	
Minus: Cost of goods sold	
= Gross profit	Gross margin
Minus: Operating expenses	
= Operating profit	Operating margin
Plus or Minus: Other Income or Expense	
= Pretax profit	Pretax margin
Less: Income tax liability	
= Net profit	Net return

FIGURE 8.1 Income Statement Labels

bottom line
the last value on the income statement, representing the earnings after all operating costs and expenses, interest, and taxes have been deducted from revenues.

both income statements and selected financial information. Many of the key long-term ratios you will need can be found in these statements or on separate financial highlights that the corporate website provides.

A key trend, of course, is the growth in revenues and related earnings. One potential problem is in finding these forms of information by segment. Many corporations have dissimilar lines of business, each with its own separate market and profitability attributes. In these instances, it is a common practice to include a detailed breakdown on yearly revenues and earnings by operating unit (also called *segment, affiliate,* or *subsidiary*).

The following four major trends are the most important on the income statement:

1. *Growth in revenues.* Among all of the fundamental indicators, revenues command more interest than any others, even earnings. A widespread belief states that as long as revenues continue to

expand, the company is healthy, even if earnings do not follow. This belief is wrong, because revenue expansion is only worthwhile if profits remain strong as well. There is a tendency during periods of revenue expansion to allow profits to diminish, and even to experience net losses. Revenue expansion is not a good cause if, as part of the price of that expansion, earnings are eroded. This is why reviewing revenues is only a part of the overall task of analyzing the income statement. You need more.

operating profit

the profit after costs and expenses are deducted from revenues but not counting "other" income and expenses such as interest, capital gains and losses, or currency exchange, and also not counting liability for income taxes.

Key Point

Higher revenue is a positive trend—unless earnings are flat or falling at the same time. If that is happening, what good are those higher revenues?

pretax profit

the net profit after all costs and expenses are deducted from revenues, before deducting liability for federal, state, or local income taxes.

2. *Gross profit margin.* Revenue expansion may also mean reduction in gross profit. The gross profit margin is a good indicator to track whether the revenue/cost relationship is remaining the same while revenues expand. It should, as long as the mix of business is constant as well. If and when a corporation acquires a new affiliate, or sells off an old one, the change might affect the gross profit margin; so when you see a change in the margin (gross profit divided by revenues, expressed as a percentage) before you conclude that something has gone wrong, check the acquisition and sale activity for the year; that might explain the change.

Key Point

Costs should track related revenues; but be careful to allow adjustments when the mix of business changes from one year to the next. That might also affect gross margin.

3. *Expenses in relation to revenues.* Another area likely to grow during periods of revenue is expansion is expenses. This group includes selling expenses as well as general and administrative expenses (overhead). Generally speaking, management is supposed to be able to keep expense expansion to a minimum even when revenues are growing. As a company expands into new territory, opens new offices, hires more employees, and pays to advertise its products, higher expenses are unavoidable. A valuable indicator is to compare expenses to revenues and track the percentage. It is reasonable to expect that expenses represent either a fixed percentage of revenues or, if they change at all, it should be to become a smaller percentage. When expenses outpace revenues, it is a sign of poor management—unless the trend is explained and that explanation makes sense. (Higher expenses in a single year could be explained as a nonrecurring but necessary change due to expansion.) The worst of all situations—but one that is not uncommon—is to experience rising revenues, rising costs (thus, shrinking gross profits), and rising expenses. If a company's profits are falling or if it is reporting net losses, why should expenses be on the rise? There is no reasonable explanation, and it would be a highly negative condition.

Key Point

When expenses outpace revenues, there is a big problem. All slick explanations aside, when expenses increase too quickly, it means management is not doing its job.

---

4. *Operating profit margin.* When costs and expenses are deducted from revenues, you end up with the operating profit or net profit. This dollar value, divided by revenues, gives you the operating profit margin. Why focus on this rather than on the after-tax net profit? The operating profit margin identifies the recurring, core earnings of the company. While the EPS is most likely based on the bottom line, you will often see two versions of EPS, one for the operating EPS and the other for the net EPS. The distinction can be important. When corporations report large gains from the sale of a segment or from capital assets, or

when its profits are affected by interest payments on long-term debt, not to mention tax liabilities, the difference between operating profit and net profit can be significant.

Key Point

Make sure the EPS numbers you use to compare between companies are based on the same numbers. If one uses operating profit and the other uses net profit, you may have two very different bases for comparison.

Insights into Expansion Period Trends

Expansion is considered a positive trend, and that is usually true. You expect corporate revenues to expand as part of the long-term growth curve. So much can go wrong during the expansion period that it is worth taking a critical look at some of the problems companies encounter when their revenues begin to grow.

Typically, these problems involve cash flow, profitability, or both, and include:

1. *Increased accounts receivable and bad debts.* As revenues grow, you expect to see a corresponding growth in the levels of accounts receivable and bad debts. These trends are unavoidable; more revenues translate to more customers and higher volume of sales. Yet in following these trends, the required control is that the levels of growth should track revenue and earnings levels. This is where cash flow problems may emerge.

    Assume, for example, that revenues have grown by 15 percent over the past three years, and that accounts receivable balances have also grown at about 12 to 15 percent. Because the increase is lower than revenues, it appears to be under control—but what about earnings? The real test should be twofold. First, the *rate* of growth should be at or below growth in revenues. Second, the dollar amount of growth should not exceed net earnings. If the growth in accounts receivable does exceed earnings, cash flow problems will likely be more severe in the future. Here is one exception: If the distortion between accounts receivable and net earnings is a seasonal problem that will be corrected later, the cash flow strain is not permanent. Also remember that earnings are not always in cash. Due to the noncash expense of depreciation, there may be more cash available than it appears by simply reviewing the income statement.

A similar rule relates to the reserve for bad debts and corresponding bad debt expense. The percentage of the reserve to the asset should remain constant; and the actual written off bad debts should also be kept in check. Companies have a high degree of control over these trends, which require diligent tracking and follow-up. If during periods of growth collection controls are relaxed, bad debts will rise and the company will begin writing off more bad debts.

2. *Higher inventory levels, with potential inefficiency.* Another consequence of growth is the need to keep ever-higher inventory on hand. This is especially true for any company involved in production of tangible goods for sale. As inventory levels increase, it is possible that management will become more inefficient. This means more capital tied up in stocks of goods, and that may also lead to loss, theft or damage, and obsolescence. The higher the inventory level, the more control is needed; and in periods of expansion, the tendency is to relax internal controls. Because of this problem, it is possible that both earnings and cash flow will weaken.

3. *A slipping gross margin due to out-of-control cost expansion.* Growth is not all positive; it often means the need for higher levels of direct costs. These include merchandise purchases for resale and corresponding inventory maintenance, and higher direct labor in cases where production or assembly is involved in the sales process.

The previously mentioned inventory inefficiency creates problems in control, storage space, and even direct labor. The higher a company's inventory, the higher the need for people to manage that inventory. Some forms of expansion also require growth in direct labor, especially in production processes. The process becomes more complex, which in turn increases labor costs and the need for internal controls. Increased idle time and inefficiency leads to higher direct costs. This shows up in deterioration of gross margin.

4. *Rapid growth in expenses.* Perhaps the most frequent problem in any corporation is the tendency for expenses to go out of control. This is most extreme during periods of growth, although unexplained higher expenses may also be seen while revenues and earnings are on the decline.

　　The higher expense problem during expansion periods is, to some degree, unavoidable. Yet expenses can be held to a reasonable level so that expansion does, in fact, translate to the bottom line. Ideally, the rate of growth in expenses should be far lower than that of revenues, ensuring improvement in the dollar amount of earnings. It is a matter of well-executed internal controls, so tracking expenses trends is an effective way to judge management's abilities.

5. *A failure to recognize the difference between profitable expansion and unprofitable expansion.* Every management team makes mistakes, and even during periods of expansion the consequences can be to incur large net losses. The myth that expansion is always good can be easily dispelled. Just look at a company's record and you may see the problems that come from unprofitable expansion. The mistake, however, is not in making errors, but in failing to identify the differences and to prevent them in the future. So many companies seek higher market share in several markets, without also considering the likelihood that higher revenues will end up on the bottom line. This can be an expensive mistake. It will show up in net losses and, finally, in the stock's market price as well.

Key Point

You look for fundamental information in a variety of places. A failure by management to back away from an ill-advised course may be as important as being able to create and maintain profits.

　　Expansion costs money and, inevitably, both costs and expenses are likely to grow along with revenues. Investors and corporate managers need to accept higher costs and expenses as part of growth; but there are distinct and specific differences between necessary higher costs or expenses, and wasteful or poorly controlled trends. Following the whole range of revenues, costs, expenses, and operating profit reveals the trends that over time help you to identify those well-managed companies that you want to own for many years versus the ones that experience growth in short periods of time—and ultimately lose money for their investors.

Relationship between Revenues and Net Earnings

In any type of analysis, the tests that reveal the most involve a study of relationships between accounts. On the income statement, the most important relationship is that between revenues and net earnings.

As a general observation, you should expect to see a company's revenues increase over time. This is achieved through one of five methods:

1. *Increased market share.* If a corporation is competing effectively, it will be able to take market share away from its competitors. It is interesting to observe how competing corporations vie for first, second, or third place and how revenues change over time. In retail, for example, any long-term observer has noted that Sears and K-Mart have been losing sales, forced to close stores, and reporting less and less retail square footage each year. In comparison, competitors Wal-Mart and Target have been expanding at the same time, dominating their markets and reporting ever-higher retail square feet. From the analytical point of view, it is sensible to observe these comparative trends; figure out what corporations are doing to compete, and how effectively they accomplish their goals; and what likely future trends should be expected.

2. *Increased market size.* Some markets grow, whereas others do not. For example, in the early 1990s there was virtually no market for Internet-based book sales or auctions. By the end of the decade, these markets had exploded. Today, most people have home computers and Internet access and a large amount of transactions take place online. This is a recent example of an expanding market. It occurs elsewhere; when auto manufacturing began more than 100 years ago, there were few useable roads or mechanics. A decade later, over 200 auto manufacturers competed for a rapidly expanding market of American consumers, demanding automobiles. Market observers know that new technology creates new markets.

3. *Mergers and acquisitions.* In the past, merger and acquisition activity was quite high. Markets have gone through phases of leveraged buyouts and the use of mergers to create favorable financial results. Aside from these strategic reasons for mergers, there is also a competitive reason. Corporations may buy smaller competitors to eliminate them as well as to expand their own market share. A well-timed and carefully structured acquisition or merger can help improve overall financial performance and justify the cost of purchasing another company. Even so, there are only so many competitors worthy of buying; so if a corporation is undergoing a large volume of mergers and acquisitions, it should raise your suspicions. Also, in attempting to estimate long-term revenues based on current trends, remember that acquisition-based revenue growth is not going to recur every year.

4. *Product line diversification.* Just as investors are encouraged to diversify their capital, corporations also need to diversify their product or service lines, for several reasons. First, diversification helps protect corporate cash flow against cyclical change. Second, it opens up new markets and helps continue healthy revenues and earnings trends. Third, diversification may become necessary when a product becomes obsolete. For example, Altria Corporation has expanded away from its previously dominant domestic tobacco sales as U.S. opposition to smoking has had an effect on sales. Altria's international tobacco sales and food division revenues are gradually replacing cigarette sales in the United States.

5. *Geographic expansion.* Corporations can open outlets overseas. The global economy is becoming more typical and less of an oddity today, compared to the past. Many corporations are already multinational in nature and international revenues represent major portions of overall revenues. While some industries are dominated by Asian corporations (notably in manufacturing and related industries), there remain many others such as retail, energy, and IT (information technology), that continue to expand overseas rapidly. International markets present potentially high revenues growth for many corporations. For investors, identifying industries likely to benefit from increased international activity, and then finding the corporations likely to benefit the most, is a sound way to choose companies for long-term expansion.

All of these sources for higher revenues are finite. No growth can continue forever without slowing down and eventually ceasing. This is a reality in any analysis of long-term revenues and earnings. So even in the most successful instance, and even when corporations employ all of the methods listed above to create and continue revenue expansion, there is a natural limit. Successful companies evolve with changing times, to take advantage of ever-growing markets. History shows this to be the case.

IBM was originally founded as a typewriter repair company. For many years IBM dominated repair and manufacturing of manual and electric typewriters. When it became apparent that the home computer would soon replace typewriters, IBM quickly reinvented its primary revenues model, replacing typewriter manufacturing with a new product line: computer hardware.

Similar examples can be found in virtually all industries. Prudential used to be known primarily for its whole life insurance business, as well as other insurance products. Today, Prudential is one of the major financial advisory concerns, with services ranging from investment banking to research, financial planning, and other related services in addition to insurance. Today, many large banks also are involved in financial services and investments as related service areas.

In retail many interesting trends are underway. The standalone franchises of the past are now found in growing numbers in larger stores or opened in combination with other franchises. Starbucks Coffee has hundreds of stores, but new franchises open up as often as not in grocery stores or in combination with other food franchises. Food courts in malls, highway access areas, and even downtown centers are seeing more and more combination Taco Bell and Burger King outlets in single buildings and fast food attached to service station convenience stores. These combinations cut overhead while exposing the stores to good volumes of traffic.

These marketing trends are examples of emerging strategic planning, taking advantage of high-volume traffic areas with reduced or low overhead setup. Even so, revenues are only one half of the revenues-earnings equation. While there are many ways to increase revenues over time, earnings may grow, but have greater limitations.

Each industry tends to experience a relatively narrow range of earnings, normally expressed as a percentage of revenues. So if a likely *range* of earnings is going to be between 12 and 15 percent of revenues, it is not rational to anticipate ever-expanding earnings growth beyond the 15 percent range.

> ### Key Point
>
> Expect growth in revenue dollar amounts and maintenance of earnings within an acceptable range. Do not impose unrealistic expectations, or you are sure to be disappointed.

Even as corporate revenues expand, costs are going to be fairly fixed and expenses can be kept at the same level only to a degree. As a result, you can realistically expect the margin to remain within the likely range in comparison to revenues. But as long as the dollar amount of revenues continues to expand, earnings will grow in dollar amount over time. A 15 percent return of $100 million in revenues is $15 million in earnings; the same 15 percent on $200 million of revenues will be $30 million in earnings—same percentage, but greater dollar amount.

Important Ratios

Three key income statement ratios should always be reviewed. Tracking these three helps you to identify well-managed corporations and to quickly eliminate those not meeting the basic test. In the following sections are two examples represented by two different companies, the Boyd's Collection and Sears.

The Boyd's Collection

As an example of a company whose ratios reflect poor performance, check the Boyd's Collection as shown in Table 8.1.

For several years, Boyd's—a corporation specializing in the business of limited edition collectibles, notably its Boyd's Bears lines—has been experiencing declining sales in a limited market. Table 8.1 shows results for four quarters ending with the first quarter of 2005. All of these dollars are in millions, so most recent quarterly revenues were $18.533 million, for example.

Note the deterioration in both gross profit and expenses. The first two quarters of the year reported showed gross profit of 61 percent; the most recent declined to 48 percent and then to 45 percent. Expenses have varied considerably, ranging from a low of 35 percent of sales (quarter ending September, 2004) to a high of 72 percent (quarter ending

TABLE 8.1 The Boyd's Collection (in millions)				
Period Ending	*31-Mar-05*	*31-Dec-04*	*30-Sep-04*	*30-Jun-04*
Total Revenue	18.533	21.916	32.835	22.626
Cost of Revenue	10.131	11.314	12.962	8.728
Gross Profit	8.402	10.602	19.873	13.898
Selling General and Administrative	10.701	13.582	11.556	11.765
Nonrecurring	2.600	—	—	—
Others	—	(4)	—	—
Total Operating Expenses	13.301	13.578	11.556	11.765
Operating Income or Loss	(4.899)	(2.976)	8.317	2.133
Total Other Income/Expenses Net	(124)	550	131	(18)
Earnings Before Interest And Taxes	(5.023)	(2.426)	8.448	2.115
Interest Expense	2.184	1.216	1.147	1.093
Income Before Tax	(7.207)	(3.642)	7.301	1.022
Income Tax Expense	70.085	(1.295)	2.836	496
Net Income	(77.292)	(2.347)	4.465	526

March, 2005). In spite of the reported high profit of $8.317 million in the September quarter, the company's revenues and earnings have been slipping for the past four or five years.

Several aspects of this report should raise eyebrows. Beginning at the top, revenues appear to be sliding—from a high of over $32 million to the more recent low of $18 million per quarter. This slip reflects the same longer-term decline over a number of years. However, while revenues decline, both costs and expenses continue to rise. This is a troubling record of financial weakness and the trend is not at all promising.

The fundamental tests performed here take two forms. The most revealing is the quarterly comparison of gross profit and expenses over four quarters. A similar test of annual results would reveal a similar slide over time. The second form of testing is application of traditional tests for each quarter. For example, in the most recent quarter, a gross profit of 45 percent of revenues is accompanied by an expense level equal to 72 percent of sales. The resulting is −26 percent. A critical review would lead most people to be troubled about the high expenses, not just based on revenues and gross profit, but also in comparison to past quarters (and past years). Why did the company report 35 percent expenses to revenues when those revenues were over $32 million, and 72 percent expenses to revenues when revenues fell to $18 million?

Key Point

Higher expenses on lower revenues—a tough one to explain—is actually not at all difficult to understand. The company is not being well managed; it is as simple as that. In a well-managed company, when revenues fall, management is supposed to reduce expenses . . . not spend more.

One possible explanation is that some expenses or revenues have been reported in the wrong period, which in itself is alarming. Another, more likely problem, is that the company has poor internal controls, so expenses continue to rise. The volatility in revenues, gross profit, and expenses are disturbing trends, whether seen quarterly or annually.

The market for this company's products is a weak one. As a non-necessity, collectibles are vanity items; and when individual budgets tighten, these are among the first expenses to be dropped. Additionally, the manufacturing of the collectibles has been moved out of the United States to China and quality has become noticeably poor. Finally, as the company's market began weakening, it failed to diversify. A smart move when the primary product is discretionary would be to diversify into entirely dissimilar product lines. (Altria has enhanced its tobacco sales with a large food division, for example.) Instead, Boyd's bought up some of its small competitors *in the same market*, meaning that a finite, limited market could not be enhanced beyond a certain point even if Boyd's bought up competitors. These factors have contributed to the declining financial picture for Boyd's Collection over the past few years.

It is clear that companies suffering declining profitability are not strong long-term growth candidates. In the case of Boyd's, weakness on the income statement is accompanied by similar declining positions on the balance sheet. These types of problems are not limited to relatively small companies. Large corporations may suffer financial weakness as well.

Sears

Look at Table 8.2, the five-year operating results reported by Sears. This company has been losing retail space as increasing numbers of its stores have been unable to compete with Target and Wal-Mart outlets—and as much smaller stores are now able to give customers lower prices than Sears. In 2005 the value of Sears stock rose substantially, but this was due to one-time profits created as the company disposed of appreciated real estate. Its long-term retail operations have been losing ground for many years.

The first observation to make is a chronic problem relating to accounting standards. There is no uniform method for reporting results, making side-by-side comparisons impossible without a lot of research. For example, Sears has chosen to report costs and expenses together so that it is impossible from this summary—found on the company's annual report and website—to tell how much is cost and how much is expense. Furthermore, Sears has not made a distinction between its core business, which is retail, and its other operations. In fact, if Sears were to isolate its retail business only, it would be reporting a *net loss* each year. Because Sears' revenue and earnings have historically been derived from finance charges, this report cannot be accurately compared to Wal-Mart, Target, and J. C. Penney income statements for the same years.

Key Point

The fact that no one reports its operating results on the same basis makes any comparisons very difficult. It limits your ability to compare results between corporations.

Even so, the figure does reveal a general decline in earnings. With revenues growing over five years by about $2 billion in annual levels, net

TABLE 8.2 Five-Year Operating Results, Sears (in millions)

	2003	2002	2001	2000	1999
Revenues	$41,124	$41,366	$40,990	$40,848	$39,430
Costs and Expenses	39,926	39,285	39,812	38,661	37,017
Operating Income	1,198	2,081	1,178	2,187	2,413
Margin	2.9%	5.0%	2.9%	5.4%	6.1%

earnings have shown a troubling decline. Remembering that these numbers are inflated because nonretail revenues are included, the picture still looks bleak. Sears reported 6.1 percent operating profit margin in 1999. By 2003 the retailer reported less than half of that—2.9 percent.

As a fundamental analyst trying to make valid side-by-side comparisons, you have a formidable task. Because every company uses its own format for reporting, you cannot easily break out all of the numbers you need. In the case of Sears, you would be able to get breakdowns by calling the Investors Relations Department, or possibly by digging through pages of footnotes (the Sears annual report runs about 140 pages per year). But is *should* be possible to get the same information for any company by referring to a uniform reporting standard. This is a failure by the accounting and auditing industry to ensure transparency among listed companies, and any reform in this area may take many years.

Another problem arises from the fact that even the reported numbers are not reliable. Sears included its substantial income from finance charges in its revenue and earnings, even though this makes it far from comparable to other retail corporations.

Armed with the information about how unreliable corporate reporting is, these examples reveal that the application of a few sensible fundamental tests can still tell you what you need to know. Declining earnings caused by ever-higher costs and expenses, weak earnings trends, or a combination of both show that when the trends are down, it does not make sense to consider the corporations as long-term growth investments. Instead, you should seek those companies that demonstrate consistent and strong growth, consistent income statement ratios, and a commanding position within its industry.

The next chapter moves beyond the financial statement and shows how some ratios are valuable when comparing price to fundamental information. The well-know PE ratio is the most popular of these, but it is only the starting point.

9

The Popular P/E Ratio and How to Use It

Never invest your money in anything that eats or needs repainting.
—Billy Rose, *New York Post*, 1957

The price/earnings ratio, or P/E, is perhaps the most popular measurement of a stock's value. As a fundamental indicator, it serves another purpose: equating fundamental and technical value in a single test.

Most analysts favor one side or the other, but the P/E involves both sides, so it demonstrates via the *multiple* (the P/E value, or multiple of earnings represented by the current price) the actual value of future profits to shareholders.

The multiple is widely acknowledged as the defining comparative feature of a stock. A high multiple means the stock is well regarded, and a low multiple means investors are less impressed. This widely held view is flawed for two reasons. First, the years of earnings reflected in the P/E are not returned to investors except for relatively small dividends; most profits are used to fund on-

> **multiple**
> in the P/E ratio, the outcome; the number of times current earnings are reflected in the price per share of stock.

going operations, retire debt, or to build reserves. Second, history has shown that lower P/E stocks outperform higher P/E stocks and do so consistently.

Key Point
The P/E ratio is a valuable and popular tool. Its actual meaning is debatable, however, and its value and importance may not be what most people perceive.

Even with these flaws, the P/E is a powerful comparative tool. Investors may identify a range or cutoff point for determining which stocks fit one of many criteria. For example, you may decide that you will only buy stocks with P/E at or below 20, meaning earnings are represented at a multiple of 20 times in the current price. Most would agree that P/E below 20 is midlevel or even on the low side. Without any doubt, exceptionally high P/E stocks are higher risk, and the higher the P/E the more likely that the stock is overvalued.

Development of the P/E

It is a worthwhile exercise to consider the actual significance of comparing price to earnings and to review its calculation. P/E is found by dividing the current price per share by the latest known earnings per share (EPS).

$$Price \div EPS = P/E$$

The price is the current price of the stock; and since price may change frequently, P/E is an everchanging ratio as well. Earnings is more elusive because the number is published only periodically, so when you use the P/E you are comparing today's stock price to earnings that may be far out of date, perhaps by as much as three months. With this in mind, giving value to the P/E should be done cautiously; it may be more revealing to study the P/E trend. Compare price as of the closing date of a quarterly financial statement to earnings as of the same date, and use the trend as a means for judging the stock's value.

EPS is not an exact value. Because the latest published earnings may reflect a specific seasonal high or low point for the company, using outdated earnings in the P/E calculation can be quite inaccurate. A retail concern's fourth quarter may reflect exceptionally high earnings due to high volume in the holiday season. By February, however, volume will be considerably lower. Thus, comparing a February price to December 31 earnings is anything but reliable.

You may recognize not only a long-term trend in P/E by matching historical dates. This also enables you to judge the stock's value based on annual cycles and cyclical changes the company undergoes as the year progresses.

The number of shares used in the calculation of EPS may further distort the value of the P/E. If the company has issued shares during the year, calculation of EPS should be based on the average shares issued and outstanding during the period the earnings reflect. If new shares are issued exactly halfway through the year, the average is easy to figure. Add the beginning and ending balances, and divide by two. However, if shares were issued on more than one date, or whenever shares are issued during the year, it is necessary to weight the calculation to reflect an accurate average for the full period.

To average shares accurately, multiply the number of shares outstanding by the percentage of the year issue date to end of the year. For example, a corporation had outstanding shares of 12,500,000 and issued additional shares three times throughout the year:

	Shares	*Months/Year*	*Multiple*
Balance January 1	12,500,000	12/12	12,500,000
Issued March 15	2,000,000	9.5/12	1,583,333
Issued July 15	1,000,000	5.5/12	458,333
Issued September 1	9,000,000	4/12	3,000,000
Balance, December 31	24,500,000		17,541,666

In this example the accurate average number of shares outstanding during the year was 17,551,666. If earnings for the year were $27,446,404, the EPS would be:

$$\$27,446,404 \div 17,551,666 = \$1.56$$

If the price per share at year-end was $23.50, then the P/E would be:

$$\$23.50 \div \$1.56 = 15$$

Calculating the P/E is not difficult; it is often included in research reports and published stock pages. The problem, however, is that you have no way of knowing what data were used. As a consequence, you cannot know whether stock-to-stock comparisons or even historical information is reliable. Both sides—price and earnings—may be inaccurate based on three important possible problems:

1. *The age of the earnings information.* Today's P/E may include current price but outdated earnings information. For example, if you are reviewing data on March 15 and the earnings were last reported on December 31, then one-half of the equation is nearly three months out of date.

2. *Subsequent restatements or adjustments.* Corporate earnings are often restated for several possible reasons. An independent audit may disagree with the published assumptions, causing a newly revised earnings summary. If the corporation has subsequently acquired a new subsidiary or sold off a previously owned operating segment, then all earnings have to be revised to conform to the current status (which also reflects current price).

3. *The timing of the price level versus today's price.* The published price side of the P/E equation may also be out of date, especially in published documents. If the price has moved several points in either direction since the P/E was published, then it is also out of date.

Given the complexity of timing for P/E, the ratio is not reliable as a current indicator in most situations. P/E is best used as part of a long-term trend, in which the price *and* earnings are reported on the same day, such as end of the fiscal quarter; adjusted for subsequent restated earnings; and then tracked over time.

Key Point

The popular use of P/E—based on current price and outdated earnings—can be highly misleading. A long-term approach using consistent data makes more sense.

Given the tendency for cyclical changes during the year, looking at a quarter-end price and earnings summary may be unreliable as well. Thus, P/E may be studied over a number of quarters or years as a *range* of levels. Standard & Poor's publishes a STARS Report available at http://www .schwab.com as well as at other sites that reports detailed fundamental and technical information for thousands of listed companies. Among the information is a range of year-end P/E ratios, both high and low, set up just like the better-known trading range of each stock. Figure 9.1 summarizes a

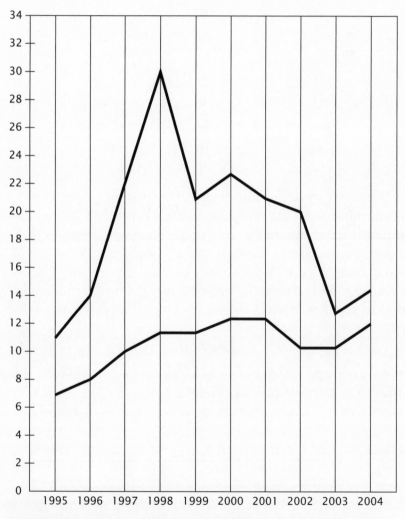

FIGURE 9.1   Citigroup P/E Range, 10 Years
Source: Standard & Poor's STARS Report.

10-year P/E range for Citigroup (trading symbol C) reported by Standard & Poor's.

To summarize the high and low P/E levels for Citigroup during the 10-year period (based on December 31 levels):

Year	High	Low
1995	11	7
1996	14	8
1997	23	11
1998	30	12
1999	21	12
2000	23	13
2001	21	13
2002	20	9
2003	14	9
2004	16	13

What can you conclude about Citigroup's long-term safety, market perception about the company, or likely future P/E trends? The 10-year record shows not only a consistently moderate range of P/E levels, but even a reduction in the most recent years in the P/E range. When this is accompanied with price range data for the same period, (which has also been fairly narrow), it becomes apparent that Citigroup has experienced very low overall volatility (in price and in P/E) over a decade.

Key Point

P/E is especially valuable when reviewed over many years and studied side-by-side with the stock's trading range.

Studying the P/E trend over many years is far more revealing than looking at P/E at a moment in time. A singular P/E level can be very deceiving, given the possibility that price moves rapidly in some cases, and earnings may be far out of date. However, studying an annual range over many years gives you a better idea of the P/E trend.

P/E Adjusted for Core Earnings

A potential problem with any ratio analysis involving the income state-ment is the possibility that large core earnings adjustments are in play. The larger the core earnings adjustments in either direction, the more critical it becomes to base long-term P/E analysis on core earnings rather than on reported earnings per share.

Standard & Poor's originated and defined core earnings and reported these values beginning in 2001. Recalculating the *core P/E ratio* is the same process as the standard P/E, except that core earn-ings are used in placed of the all-inclusive "earnings" per share. Figure 9.2 summarizes and compares net income and core earnings for the four years from 2001 and 2004 for Citigroup.

> **core P/E ratio**
> the price/earn-ings ratio using the adjusted core earnings in place of reported net earnings (or net income) used in the traditional P/E calculation.

Net earnings

Core earnings

FIGURE 9.2 Citigroup Earnings, 4 Years
Source: Standard & Poor's STARS Report.

The earnings per share are next compared to *core* earnings per share, as shown in Figure 9.3.

Key Point
Reported net earnings may be highly unreliable if a large dollar value of core earnings adjustments were made for the year. Checking core earnings as well as reported earnings is crucial for ensuring the P/E's reliability.

While the difference in EPS based on net income and core earnings per share is not significant in this example, it can be. And that's the point. To fully appreciate the long-term growth curve of earnings, it is important to make the adjustment to core earnings and to be prepared to adjust P/E if and when big shifts occur.

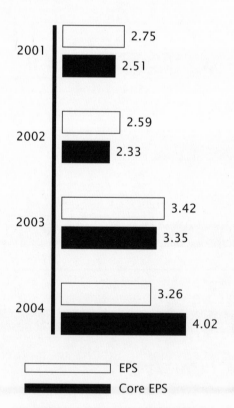

FIGURE 9.3 Citigroup EPS and Core EPS
Source: Standard & Poor's STARS Report.

The P/S Ratio

The P/E ratio is not the only important test using price (a technical indicator) and financial information. The *P/S ratio* is a comparison between a stock's price and sales (revenues). Also referred to as the revenue multiple, the P/S ratio demonstrates revenue growth in terms of market price. Although this may be inaccurate in terms of calculating future growth in earnings, it is an interesting alternative to the more popular barometer of the P/E ratio.

> **P/S ratio**
> the ratio of price per share, to sales (revenue) per share. The equation normally uses a full year's revenues per share, and is most accurate when tracked over many years.

The calculation begins with the EPS just like that used in the P/E ratio. Next, annual sales are divided by shares issued and outstanding. (The same caveat applies here as with the previous ratio: *average* shares outstanding should be calculated on the basis of issue date to arrive at a true and consistent average value.)

Key Point

Comparing price to sales is a useful confirming indicator for the P/E. It also helps track potential growth when a company has some years of net losses.

Some analysts have attempted to equate P/S levels with value of stock. For example, it has been written that a P/S level below one dollar per share represents a cheap stock. There is a significant problem with such conclusions, however. Different industries report widely diverse earnings structures. In some businesses, such as construction and retail, you expect to see a fairly low net return, usually in single digits. In other industries, you expect fairly high gross profit and net profit. For example, compare IBM (which is predominantly involved in hardware sales) and Microsoft (which reports most of its revenues on software sales) and you will see quite a big difference in the structure of the income statement and in the net return. It would be highly unrealistic to compare P/S for these two companies and describe one as undervalued and the other as overvalued. They cannot be compared based on P/S.

There are important ways that P/S can be applied, however:

1. *It provides a confirming ratio and trend to be used along with the P/E.* Every fundamental investor can benefit from confirmation. For example, if the P/S ratio remains consistent, but the P/E ratio range is rising each year, what does that mean? If revenues are not keeping pace with the change in the P/E multiple, it could indicate that the stock is overpriced. The actual P/E and P/S ranges may also be distorted by newly issued shares, so there is no absolute rule governing what P/E and P/S should track.

2. *It avoids the problem of core earnings adjustments, notably when most of those adjustments involve expenses but not revenues.* For companies with exceptionally large core earnings adjustments or significant volatility in reported earnings, the P/S ratio is particularly useful, especially as a confirming trend. So often, fundamental volatility is the result of accounting tinkering to keep earnings high when revenues are flat. In these instances, the bottom-line confusion can be cleared up by a declining trend in the P/S ratio.

3. *P/S is valuable for tracking market trends for companies that have not reported net earnings every year.* It is impossible to track P/E over time if a company has reported net losses in some years. In those cases there cannot be a P/E ratio. So lack of earnings makes long-term analysis of P/E less reliable. Here tracking revenue and price may provide a better indicator of long-term growth—assuming that the company is able to eventually establish a profitability trend and keep it moving forward.

book value per share
the value of a company, expressed on a per-share basis. The net worth is divided by the average shares issued and outstanding during the year, and the result is expressed in dollars and cents per share.

The P/B Ratio

Another price-based variation of the P/E is the ratio comparing price to *book value per share*. To make the *P/B ratio* accurate and reliable, it makes sense to use *tangible book value per share*. If you include intangible assets in the calculation, it is possible to eliminate the potential value in this ratio. Intangible assets are normally excluded from all fundamental ratios; their value is a matter of speculation, so isolating only those tangible assets makes sense. To calculate tangible book value, begin with net worth, and then subtract any intangible assets. Next, divide the *average* tangible book value per share by the number of shares issued (again, remembering to calculate a true average when newly issued shares are involved) to arrive at the P/B.

P/B ratio
price to book value per share, based on the calculation of tangible assets rather than on all assets. Price is divided by tangible net worth (net worth minus intangible assets) to arrive at the ratio, which is expressed as a numeric value.

Key Point

When comparing price to book value, remove intangible assets from total net worth to ensure accuracy.

The ratio may be further adjusted to account for core net worth adjustments. This is where the calculation may become complicated. Net worth should be adjusted to include unreported liabilities, such as long-term lease and purchase commitments and liability for future pension and profit-sharing payments. However, net worth should also be increased to report the current market value of long-term assets rather than the traditional basis minus depreciation. All of these adjustments can be significant, require estimates, and make the P/B ratio less reliable than comparisons between price and earnings (or better yet, between price and core earnings).

tangible book value per share
the book value per share, excluding all intangible assets. This is an adjustment to book value per share, in which intangible assets are subtracted from total net worth.

Key Point

Comparing price to book value is not a reliable value-based ratio by itself, or for comparisons between companies in different industries. It can be used for confirming P/E trends, however.

P/B is not useful as a comparative trend between different companies. This becomes evident whenever balance sheets are compared between industries. Some types of companies tend to have very high net worth, but they do not necessarily report higher revenue or earnings. Furthermore, asset side and net worth do not affect relative market price per share. While market price does reflect net earnings and revenues over time (and, more accurately, the growth trend), book value per share and asset or net worth size cannot be used reliably to make judgments about a stock's price, not even over many years.

P/B may be useful in comparing two companies with approximately the same net worth and functioning within the same industry—but again, the ratio should be used only to confirm or check other fundamental tests, because it is not a reliable yardstick of price performance or value. Some analysts consider P/B as a measure of efficiency, a test of net asset "turnover," or the use of assets to generate earnings per share. This is dubious when applied to dissimilar companies. The origin of asset turnover is the manufacturing sector from several decades ago and has little relevance today in most sectors of the economy. Even in manufacturing concerns, old-style *cost accounting* tests are not as relevant today as they were in the past. These tests mean less now due to outsourcing, international competition, computerization of many manufacturing processes, and vastly improved machine efficiency.

cost accounting

a type of accounting focusing on detailed analysis and study of manufacturing costs for the purpose of identifying inefficiencies and controlling unit costs of production.

The P/B ratio is useful as one of many confirming tests, but its importance should be discounted due to the complexities and variations that may affect its outcome but not actually have impact on the stock price.

P/C ratio

a comparison between a stock's current price and the company's ending balance of cash per share. This may include only cash, or the combination of cash and short-term investments in marketable securities.

The P/C Ratio

Another interesting price-based ratio is the *P/C ratio*, which compares the stock's price to cash per share. This may seem odd at first glance, because the relationship is truly remote and the ability to distort cash levels makes the ratio one of dubious value.

The calculation of "cash" may include just cash, or a combination of cash and short-term investments, notes receivable, and savings accounts. However, a corporation may easily commit itself to long-term notes or issue bonds and place proceeds in cash, which would distort the P/C ratio. The problems associated with consistency and reliability make the P/C a good measure of such distortions over time; but otherwise, its utility is limited in value.

> ### Key Point
>
> The limited value of the P/C ratio points out a common flaw in funda-mental analysis: the tendency to use ratios because someone likes them, even when they do not reveal any useful information.

The ratio may have exceptional value in certain types of industries, where the use and generation of cash has much to do with the generation of profits. For example, in financial corporations, such as insurance com-panies, the use of cash to create net investment income is a determining factor in profitability. So the P/C ratio is valuable in these types of com-panies, assuming that the related account values (especially short-term and long-term borrowing, and the balance between cash and invest-ments) remain fairly stable from year to year.

Historical Trends and What They Reveal

The various price/fundamental ratios are popular among investors be-cause they provide a bridge between technical and fundamental data. The danger is in trying to equate and judge value based on data that may not be truly comparable or that is of limited value. The purpose in such ratios is to decide whether market price of stock is high or low.

The traditional P/E ratio remains the strongest indicator for this purpose. As the earnings multiple grows, so does the likelihood that the stock is overpriced. History reveals that markets often expect too much from stocks, based on the observation that lower-P/E stocks perform bet-ter than higher P/E stocks. The remaining price-related ratios are valu-able for comparison purposes or for application in specific industries.

As valuable as the P/E may be for judging a stock's price in terms of value, it is complex. Be sure you compare P/E among companies on the same basis. The problems with P/E include timing of each side in the equa-tion, so that P/E is more valuable when fixed-time comparisons and ranges are reviewed over many years. You also need to decide whether to trust the traditional net earnings reported under the accounting rules, or make ad-justments for core earnings. The difference between reported and core earn-ings can be very significant, making standard P/E less reliable than core P/E.

So it is important to ensure that you use the same assumptions and sources of data for all versions of the P/E and other price-specific ratios. Also recognize the potential for volatility on both sides of the equation.

For example, if price varies between $30 and $40 per share in a one-month period, today's P/E can be vastly different than it was a month ago. Making investment decisions based on a specific day's P/E is an unreliable basis for the decision. Thirty dollars represents only 75 percent of the $40 price level. P/E, therefore, is likely to be affected as well. (The degree depends on the number of shares outstanding.)

Key Point

Volatility makes all short-term ratios unreliable, which is why you need to track financial trends over time, and based on broader ranges of values. No fixed-in-time ratio can be relied upon for timing of decisions.

Historical trends reveal much about price volatility and the fundamentals. P/E reflects the market's perception about a stock, so a valuable test is to compare long-term trading range with long-term P/E range. If you can adjust the P/E to use core earnings in place of traditional net earnings, the comparison becomes even more reliable. In this chapter's example, you saw that Citigroup's relatively low price volatility was confirmed by a consistently low and improving low range in year-end P/E. Because core earnings were fairly low, little change was caused by those adjustments.

If an investor was considering buying Citigroup and one important concern was volatility in price and in the fundamentals, these types of long-term range tests would be reassuring. At least they would be more than simply looking at today's reported P/E. The tests are further confirmed and checked by using P/S (price/sales), P/B (price/book value), and P/C (price/cash) ratios. Remember, however, that these secondary price tests should not be used definitively to compare different industries or stocks, but are valuable as confirming indicators. The P/S is especially useful to overcome high volatility in core earnings adjustments, or to track growth trends in companies reporting years of net loss as well as years of net gains.

The P/E and other price ratios combine fundamental and technical analysis. For this reason they are both useful and popular. However, it is important to remember that the relationship between fundamental and technical is elusive and not always accurate. This problem is the topic of the next chapter, which expands on the combination ratio and shows how fundamental trends can be confirmed with some basic technical tests.

Chapter 10

Using Fundamental— and Technical—Analysis Together

The desire of knowledge, like the thirst of riches, increases ever with the acquisition of it.
— Laurence Sterne, *Tristram Shandy*, about 1760

The two theories of analysis—fundamental and technical—each have strong proponents. In practice you can effectively employ elements of both sides to make judgments about companies and their stocks. Favoring one view over the other is a mistake—in picking stocks that match your risk tolerance, you should look at many attributes. On the fundamental side, you should consider historical returns, results of operations, capitalization, dividend history, and working capital; on the technical side, *volatility*, which is expressed by trading range and price history.

volatility
the tendency of stock prices to change or move in a trading range over time. High volatility is characterized by a broad trading range and widely varying price trends; low volatility is characterized by a narrow trading range and stable price trends.

Volatility as a Measure of Market Risk

Volatility is a key element in the technical definition of market risk. Even the most devoted fundamental analyst must be aware of a stock's price volatility and its significance. It is impossible to isolate price volatility from fundamental analysis; indeed, you should view various levels of volatility as symptoms of fundamental status. Highly volatile stocks behave as they do for several reasons, some of which go back to the fundamentals. For example, when many adjustments are made in recurring years, investors become uncertain about a company's long-term growth. Fundamental volatility, therefore, that the tendency for fundamental indicators to change significantly from year to year, may directly cause and create a stock's price volatility.

Key Point

There is a specific and distinct relationship between fundamental (financial) and technical (price) volatility, although this point is often ignored or not realized by analysts.

The most obvious value of tracking price volatility is clear: Higher-volatility stocks are higher-risk stocks and vice versa. Measurement of volatility can be accomplished in at least two ways. Simply observing a price chart provides a clear view of how volatile a stock's price history has been. A popular volatility formula based on 12-month stock price change is also used by many technicians, but caution is in order.

The formula calculates a percentage of volatility based on variation in price. The difference between a 12-month high and low is divided by the annual low to arrive at the volatility percentage:

$$(\text{High} - \text{Low}) \div \text{Low} = \text{Volatility}$$

This formula is useful for comparative analysis between stocks and also for tracking a stock's volatility over time. However, be aware that the high/low range may assume many shapes and trends, and it does not always indicate the same outcome. Here is what to look for in the following scenarios:

1. *Price trend is on the rise.* When the price trend is rising, it indicates favor in the market, which reflects well upon the fundamentals and may further be confirmation of strong operating results, working capital and capitalization, not to mention competitive strength, effective management, and favorable dividend yield.

2. *Price trend is on the decline.* An identical volatility level may have an opposite meaning. If the price has been declining for the past year, does this also confirm weakening fundamentals? If not, does it foreshadow changes yet to come? What does the falling price mean in terms of competitive position, management effectiveness, and dividend yield? In other words, *why* is the price falling?

3. *Price trend is remaining in the same range, although volatile.* A most troubling form of volatility is one in which beginning and ending price levels are similar, but the stock has traded in a wide range and price has moved around a lot during the year. Investors expect some degree of certainty in the price trend, so high volatility without much price change can be a danger signal in terms of market risk. Remember, the volatility percentage in this situation may be identical to a generally rising or falling price trend, but signal a troubling technical trend. As a fundamental investor, you want to investigate the causes of such volatility and equate those causes with the fundamental trends that you are following.

4. *Price trend may be generally low volatility, but distorted by a one-time spike.* The greatest problem with a simple volatility formula is that it does not distinguish different trading patterns. For example, consider the case of a stock with very low volatility, but whose price has a one-time spike during the last 12 months. Price may jump or fall by many points, only to return to previously established trading levels. The spike may have been caused by a rumor or outside influences. A good guideline to follow is, if the price returns to a previous trading range and remains there, then the price spike should be removed from the volatility analysis. Just as statisticians remove the aberration from their study, market analysts should do the same. The spike is not representative of the trading range, so it should not count in judging price volatility.

Price volatility is the most reliable method for quantifying market risk; use the guidelines in this section to make sound judgments because different pricing trends have to be interpreted realistically. The percentage of volatility does not have a universal meaning, nor can it be used to compare two stocks.

Employing a Combined Program

The principle of confirmation tells you that any trend should be verified and checked with the use of other trends. If you limit yourself to only fundamental analysis, you need to confirm an apparent financial trend with another; but when you also use technical indicators, you can develop an effective method for ensuring that your trends mean what they appear to mean.

Key Point
Confirmation is the critical process in determining whether to act on information you develop. Even the most obvious trend should be confirmed before you exchange money.

Examples of confirming fundamental trends with technical indicators:

1. *Volatility relationships.* The reported revenues and earnings are difficult to predict. Earnings are way up one year, followed by net operating losses the next; many one-time adjustments are appearing; noncore profits from selling assets distort earnings per share; and management seems unable to control expense levels. In this situation, when fundamental volatility makes it difficult to forecast growth, you are also likely to see increasing price volatility. Uncertainty on one side is reflected on the other.

2. *Revenue/earnings change seen in price trends.* As revenues and earnings rise, it is reasonable to see the same trend reflected in the stock's price. The same is true in the other direction; as revenues and earnings decline, stock prices are likely to confirm the trend by falling as well.

3. *Market changes seen in financial results* and *in price breakouts.* The market for an entire industry may change, causing price breakouts

for leading companies within that industry. The same is true for individual companies. For example, if a pharmaceutical company is awaiting approval of a new drug, the stock price may anticipate that approval (or a denial) even to the extent that prices break out of previously established trading ranges.

The technical may also contradict what the fundamental trends appear to reveal. The relationship between financial developments and market price are directly related, although there may be a time lag or even a predictive change on one side or the other. Here are some examples:

Key Point

Confirmation does not always mean verification; it is equally important to find contradictory information in a second indicator. That may tell you that the trend being confirmed is *not* accurate.

---

1. *Seemingly predictable financial results, but very volatile price trends.* When the fundamentals appear stable, you may assume that all is well. But what does it mean if price trends become highly volatile during the same period? It could be that undercurrents and news about a company are reflected in price instability, which may *foreshadow* the change in the fundamentals—even though that change might not show up immediately. It is reasonable to assume that "the market"—collectively the analysts, observers, investors, and institutional management that follow stocks closely—cause price volatility for good reason. The reasons do not always show up in the fundamentals first. So high price volatility may signal a trend contradicting the apparent fundamental trend in effect today.

2. *Highly volatile fundamental trends, but low price volatility.* It is possible that a company will experience high fundamental volatility but lack a confirming trend on the technical side. When the high financial volatility is not confirmed, what does it mean? It may be that the company is going through a transitional phase, expanding its product base, buying or selling operating units, changing management—all of which may cause fundamental volatility for two or three years. When prices remain

stable during such a period, it probably means that the company is perceived as remaining a strong long-term hold. The technical indicator contradicts the seemingly unstable financial side.

3. *High earnings predictions but declining market price.* What does it mean when a company predicts high earnings, but the price slides nonetheless? For the astute fundamental analyst, this could be a contradictory signal requiring more in-depth analysis of the financial results. When market price declines for a stock, meaning demand for shares is weakening, it occurs because institutional investors have lost faith in the company, or when perception states the price is too high, or when the earnings predictions are thought to be exaggerated. This contradiction should not be ignored.

4. *No obvious financial change, but sudden run-up or decline in stock price.* So much of the perception in the market does not show up in the numbers. Also, the latest known financial results are, by definition, out of date today. So even when management and Wall Street analysts are not making surprise announcements about earnings but prices change rapidly, it means that *something is going on*—and that you cannot rely solely on historical financial information to figure it out. Review current news about the company, find out why prices are changing (whether moving up or down), and equate those technical changes to fundamental sources. It is likely that the root causes will show up in the next published financial report; but the technical signs indicate that the change is already known, and you need only to look for it.

Using the Best of Both Sides

As a fundamental investor, should you simply ignore price trends, volatility, and current news or rumors? Everyone in the market realizes how impractical that would be. It makes no sense to act as a "purist" and even those who swear by the financial statement react to price news. Many of the television financial shows devote two-thirds of program time to reminding viewers that the fundamentals are what count; and the remaining time discussing price "winners and losers" and making predictions about market index movements! So these so-called fundamental adherents wind up their programming on purely technical matters.

You can make good use of both fundamental and technical indicators in combination. The definition of market risk involves price and is quantified by measurements of volatility. While some of those measurements are notoriously inaccurate (see the previous discussion), they make an important point: Fundamental investors cannot afford to ignore volatility and stock price trends.

As a balanced program, you may consider a range of both fundamental and technical indicators to follow. Picking a series of indicators achieves two important goals. First, it reduces a list of stocks you are willing to review; and second, it isolates specific risk levels and growth candidates from among a broader range of companies.

While you are likely to select your own favorite fundamental and technical indicators, consider the following list as a possible range to track. The purpose here is to limit the list to straightforward, easy-to-follow trends, involving information that is easy to locate on company websites, annual reports, financial statements, and brokerage sites:

Fundamental Indicators

Trend in revenues over many years

Gross profit margin

Net margin (based on core earnings)

Dividend yield (and consistency in increasing dividends annually)

Current ratio

Debt ratio

Combination Indicators

P/E ratio (based on core earnings per share)

P/S ratio (if company profits are inconsistent, or losses have been reported)

Technical Indicators

Trading range trends over the long term

Price high/low analysis and volatility (adjusted for spikes)

This very short list includes six fundamental, two combination, and two technical indicators. While these are by no means applicable to every situation, they cover most of the concerns that investors normally have about risk on various levels.

Should you pay attention to the broader market indices? The Dow Jones Industrial Average (DJIA), S&P 500, and NASDAQ are popular measurements of daily up-and-down movements by various measurements, weighting, and selection of stocks. While index reports do indicate overall market sentiment (i.e., bull or bear market trends), they are only one way to measure what is going on in the market. Long-term trends may exist and do influence how individual stocks behave; when sentiment is pessimistic, stocks are more likely to fall or remain flat. In terms of deciding when to take specific action, index trends provide no useful information. Marketwide trends, in contrast, may provide a general overview, but these trends do not help you to make the four important market decisions: buy, sell, hold, or stay away.

Key Point

Following popular indices is a favored pastime on Wall Street. However, when it comes to buying a particular stock, index trends are useless.

Only specific stock analysis can help; and to round out a program of analysis, you need to consider any source of information that provides insight about growth potential, risk, and timing. You have many sources available, not only from the companies directly but also from brokerage research sources. It is a mistake to rely on recommendations from any brokerage firm that also performs investment banking services, because research coming from that source is inherently defined by conflict of interest. There is no shortage of free sources of research and information, without such conflicts.

Many online brokerage services offer not only discounts on trading costs, but also free research for many corporations. These include both fundamental and technical summaries and long-term histories in many instances, as well as the brokerage firm's own rating of companies. While many brokerage services are available, one service that competes well in this respect is Charles Schwab & Company (http://www.schwab.com). Clients have access to the brokerage firm's ratings as well as S&P and Reuters opinions and ratings of various indicators for companies in comparison to its competitors.

One of the most attractive features on that site is free access to the S&P STARS Report for listed companies. This includes a multiyear price and volume charts; narrative summaries; key stock statistics; five-year reviews of revenues, earnings; dividend data; per-share data; income statement summaries; and balance sheet summaries. Subscribers to services providing this level of detail often pay hundreds of dollars per year, but it is free to clients of the brokerage service. Besides the Schwab site, many other online brokerages also offer similar free research. When comparing trading fee levels, be sure to investigate the free services offered as well; it is worth paying more for trades to also get extensive research.

Seek a brokerage firm that provides a mix of fundamental and technical information that meets most (if not all) of your requirements. This saves you time and effort and makes the task of compiling research much easier. In fact, using services like the STARS Report makes analysis virtually easy. Also look for research that, like the S&P service, breaks down earnings and EPS on the basis of *core* earnings. Because that distinction was defined and instituted by S&P, it is part of the analysis for each stock included in the service, on an overall basis as well as on a per-share basis.

Using Technical Tests as Confirmation of the Fundamentals

Technical tests not only expand your analytical range; they also help you to identify relative risks among a series of stocks. Remember, the higher the price volatility, the greater the market risk. Including such tests also helps you to confirm ongoing fundamental tests.

The various methods of confirmation help you to place fundamental trends in perspective. All forms of trend analysis are likely to contain false indicators, misleading directions, and the possibility that information will be misinterpreted. Confirmation as practiced under the Dow Theory requires that indicated movement in one index be tracked by movement in the same direction by another index. This is true not only to establish a primary trend, but also to signal the conclusion and reversal of that trend.

Key Point

All trends may include false starts and misleading signals. This is why the technical side is so valuable—technical indicators are excellent tools for confirmation of fundamental trends.

The same insight can be derived in the use of technical tests to confirm what the fundamentals reveal. In setting a new trend, changes may be subtle and difficult to spot immediately. Technical trends may follow the fundamental shift or even precede it. Because price—the dominant factor in technical analysis—is chaotic in the short term, it is difficult to reply on immediate price changes, with one exception: when price movements signal a major change as defined under technical rules. These changes are signaled by:

1. *Breakouts.* Prices are expected to remain within an established trading range and, in technical terms, this is an established trend. The range may be gradually increasing in price range, or falling, but the distance between high and low price remains about the same. As long as the distance of the range is about the same, the trend continues. When prices move suddenly above the resistance level or below support level, it is called a breakout. If the breakout is sustained, it signals the end of the previous trading range and establishment of a new range at a higher or lower level.

2. *Gaps.* Technicians normally expect a day's opening price to exist somewhere between the previous day's high and low. So if yesterday's trading was between 25 and 28 points, you would expect today's opening price to be within the same level. Occasionally, a small gap is established and, if isolated, it does not matter. This is called a *common gap* and does not signal any particular trend. Three other types are more meaningful, however. A *breakaway gap* involves not only price movement above or beyond previously established levels, but also outside of the established trading range. A *runaway gap* involves accelerating, multiple movements away from trading range over several days.

common gap
chart pattern involving a space between the previous trading range and a new opening price; an insignificant adjustment in a stock's price range.

Finally, an *exhaustion gap* occurs at the end of the price breakout, signaling a reversal (recognizable only in hindsight).

All of the gap patterns are useful for recognizing changes in market risk. However, of equal interest to the fundamental analyst is equating the sudden change in stock price with a fundamental root cause. Price gaps occur for a reason, and when they do occur, it may be traced to fundamental news or earnings reports. Such gaps are particularly useful when they precede announcements of fundamental change. For the longer-term fundamental analyst, short-term gap patterns are not always of great concern; but strong price movement that lasts for several days or weeks can be important in terms of fundamental change, and such patterns can be used to put yourself on alert for emerging financial news and trends.

3. *Patterns testing support or resistance.* The gap is a signal that previously establishing trading ranges are no longer valid. But trading ranges can also be tested. Technicians point to head and shoulders patterns in which either resistance (top pattern) or support (bottom, or reverse pattern) are tested. The pattern involves three high or low price peaks, with the second peak exceeding the level of the first and third. The pattern is considered significant because, as the theory states, the three tests of the resistance or support levels signal a price movement in the opposite direction. While short-term price *trends* are not reliable for identifying short-term price *movement*, the technical head and shoulders pattern often does precede price changes going down (after top head and shoulders) or up (after bottom head and shoulders), and signals a change in the trading range.

breakaway gap
a sudden movement in a stock's price involving space between past and current trading range *and* also above or below the established trading range.

runaway gap
an extreme price gap pattern in which a series of recurring gaps moving above or below previously established trading range signals an important change in the stock's trading levels.

exhaustion gap
the conclusion of a period of strong price movement, in which the gap pattern precedes a reversal in the gap-specific price change. The exhaustion gap is recognizable only in hindsight.

These are the basic technical patterns. Many highly specialized technical systems are in use, some highly complex and based on mathematical formulas or patterns. Their applicability is debatable, but many people believe in them. A recommendation worthy of your fundamental program: Limit your dependence on technical indicators to the basics, and avoid the more complex theories.

Key Point

A common mistake is to watch too many indicators. Whether you use fundamental or technical tests, keep the list short, but effective. Otherwise you will drown in information and be unable to make any decisions.

In reversing a previously established trend, technical indicators can also be very informative. A lot of emphasis is placed on how indicators (fundamental or technical) serve to signal the beginning of a trend. It is just as important to be able to recognize when the trend begins to slow down and reverse itself. For the purely fundamental analysis of trends, you may recognize that a strong existing trend in earnings may begin to soften when revenues start to flatten out; this is a classic interpretation and a reliable one as well. However, technical trends may be equally valuable in confirming or anticipating the end of established trends.

Recognizing that both fundamental and technical indicators can be useful is a wise and perceptive approach to managing your portfolio. This is especially the case for identifying trend reversals. It has been said that timing is everything; most people identify with this in terms of buying a stock just before its price begins to rise. Those same people, however, may have little idea about when or if they should sell their stock. Short-term speculation involves timing on both the buy and sell sides; but long-term investors also need to be aware of timing and identify when a hold changes to a sell signal.

Examples of technical signals may include a slowing down in the rate of price growth, a change in the trading range (either narrowing or widening), or changes in daily trading volume. It is not enough to make a decision to sell solely on the basis of price or volume trends, even though many investors do make that mistake. Remember, the short-term trend is not reliable as the basis for making decisions; but it may be most useful as a generator of diligent fundamental research. This is based on the premise that prices change for good reasons and the belief that while short-term pricing is chaotic, technical trends emerge for fundamental reasons. These reasons involve slowly emerging fundamental trends in revenues, earnings, and capitalization and should not be ignored.

Even if you have great devotion to a particular company and its stock, be aware that today's status may change in the future. Thus, following the fundamental indicators is essential, but it is not always the full story. When you think about many of the past market icons that have fallen on hard times, the point is well taken. General Motors has always been thought of as a leading established American company. However, by 2005, the company was in deep trouble. Unbooked pension liabilities exceeded GM's net worth. Many previously strong companies have filed bankruptcy, including several big airlines, retail stores, and well-established industry leaders such as Polaroid. Other well-known corporations were discovered to have been cooking their books in one way or another, including Sunbeam and Xerox.

The point to be made here is that fundamental and technical indicators can work together to provide you with powerful, insightful views of emerging trends. Price trends do not occur in a vacuum but are a response to (or anticipation of) fundamental change, and can be used to identify both positive and negative fundamental changes.

The next chapter expands on the idea of using indicators besides fundamentals. If you limit your analysis to only the balance sheet and income statement, you gain only part of the larger picture. You also need to consider that economic, political, and other outside influences may affect a company's fortunes—and that your investment value can change as a result.

Indicators That Go beyond the Statements

Cynics know the answers without having penetrated deeply enough to know the questions. When challenged by mysterious truths, they marshal "facts."
—Marilyn Ferguson, *The Aquarian Conspiracy*, 1980

Financial statements are just part of the whole story. As presented in the annual report, it is the corporate "best face" put forward to impress investors, analysts, and institutional managers. There is more.

Even within the annual report, narrative sections are meant to portray a company in the most positive manner and to assure existing shareholders that the future is promising—even following up on a dismal year of lower sales and net losses. Given the public relations theme to virtually every annual report, how can you look beyond the balance sheet and income statement to find the real signals about a company's health?

While distant economic indicators, political trends, and other nonfinancial trends can serve as fundamental signals, they—like each financial ratio—are useful only as confirming indicators. You cannot pick stocks based on which party wins a presidential election, which league wins the World Series, or the spaces between tree rings. Even so, illogical theories like these feed popular Wall Street myths and persist over time.

Key Point
Odd and irrational theories cannot be supported with facts. Even so, they persist and have become primary forces in American investing markets.

Among the most favored myth in the investment world is the idea that market direction can somehow be anticipated through unassociated indicators. While such ideas are found mainly on the technical side, where many illogical market theories abound, even fundamental analysts may be distracted by this "magical thinking." Examples of this tendency include wearing a lucky hat when attending a sports event, believing that it will make your team win (or, more likely, wearing a different hat would cause the team to lose). Such thinking has no place in the market, where your decisions involve the possibility of risking large sums of money; here you need to depend on science, hard work, and a well-grounded appreciation of cause and effect. If you identify the strong fundamental attributes of a company, both on and off its financial statements, you increase your chances for profits and reduce the risks of investing.

Magical thinking depends on illogical and misleading nonfundamental indicators. When an effect resembles the root causes, it is easy to mistake the similarity for a *fact* when it is actually a coincidence. Logic explains these phenomena but magic thinking is compelling. If you observe that the market rises every four years when one political party wins and falls when the other party wins, does that make the trend a law? Of course, there may be economic cause and effect at work, but the similarity in the trend is more likely to be the effect of economic conditions than the cause.

Key Point
Magical thinking allows you to believe that wishful thinking, secret systems, or simple good luck can help you beat the market. And why not? That is less work than actually analyzing the numbers.

It makes sense for technical investors to develop respect for the fundamentals; ignoring financial health and operating trends is a mistake. By the same argument, fundamental investors can gain insight and confirming information by observing technical trends. Both sides can also look beyond the limited universes in which these schools of thought operate and find meaningful indicators in other places. Some guidelines for all investors:

1. *Recognize the difference between factual and whimsical information.* Whenever the chance exists for anyone to make a lot of money, two elements are ever present. First is the tendency to focus on the profit opportunity and ignore risk. Second is the confusion between fact and fiction. Keep a clear distinction in your mind between reality and magical thinking. Many investors react to promises of quick and easy riches; but there is no such thing as a system that will help you beat the market. Again, it just takes hard work, fact-finding, and identification of investing opportunities.

2. *Respect fundamental as well as technical science, but avoid get-rich-quick schemes.* There are plenty of ideas out there, but none of them will actually help you to make a fortune without any work. Many appeals for subscription services, secret formulas, and magical answers appeal to the human desire to get rich without having to work at it. But these ideas never work, and logic tells us that.

3. *Keep an open mind, but always ask the same basic question.* There may be variations on analysis that provide you with some insight into how value develops within companies, or how current trends begin to change. So keeping an open mind helps you to continuously learn more about how to invest. At the same time, always ask yourself: "Does this theory make sense logically?" That has to be the basic question, the one that helps you avoid trouble and to stay focused on logic.

Key Point

Fundamental investors tend to use logic, self-discipline, and intelligence to make informed decisions. For this reason, they also tend to earn higher profits than speculators and technicians.

Asking the right questions helps you to avoid distractions and misdirection. You seek logical, intelligent methods for picking well-managed companies. Among the many fundamental indicators taken from financial statements that help you do this is the dividend history. It is one of the most important indicators available and a good starting point for any fundamental program.

The Importance of Dividend History

Dividend yield and dividend history can act as selection criteria for stocks. Those corporations that pay better than average dividends, and that are able to increase dividends every year, also tend to be the best-managed corporations in their industries.

Dividend yield (also called "current yield") is one of the most misunderstood of fundamental indicators. Some investors believe the yield is fixed; but in fact, it varies based on the price you pay for stock. As the stock price declines, dividend yield rises. For example, if a stock sold last month for $55 per share and dividends were 45 cents per share ($1.80 per share for the full year), then dividend yield was 3.27%, what happens when the stock's price falls to $48? The answer:

$$\$1.80 \div \$48 = 3.75\%$$

Dividend yield, calculated based on current share price, should be used as a means for comparison only when you have not yet purchased shares. Once you buy shares, your actual yield is always going to be based on (1) dividends declared and paid, and (2) your original price per share of stock. No matter how much the stock's market value changes after purchase, your dividend yield remains the same. If you look in the daily newspaper or online listings, you will find the current yield for each stock; this does not matter except at the time you make your purchase.

Key Point

Dividend yield—annual payments divided by the price of shares—is significant only as it relates to your purchase price. Once prices move after your purchase, reported yields do not affect your situation.

With the understanding of what dividend yield actually means, you can use both yield and the company's history of increasing dividend payments for many years, as a way to pick stocks. When corporations increase dividends each year over many years, this is one attribute of sound management. These "dividend achievers" also tend to display other important attributes:

1. *They tend to have lower than average price volatility.* The trading range of well-managed corporations tends to be fairly narrow, compared to average trading ranges.

2. *These companies also display lower than average core earnings adjustments.* The degree and amount of core earnings adjustments—for noncore revenues, costs, and expenses—tends to be lower than average companies' similar adjustments each year.

3. *Finally, financial statements and history reveal low fundamental volatility.* Perhaps most revealing of all, well-managed companies tend to have predictable growth in revenue and earnings. The fact that dividend payments grow from year to year is often mirrored in greater financial predictability.

The selection of stocks is never a simple matter; an excellent way to narrow down the list of candidates is on the basis of consistency in dividend payments. Mergent offers a subscription service for Dividend Achievers, including a quarterly publication that studies corporation in depth with 10-year or greater history of increasing dividend payments. Mergent also has devised and organized the Dividend Achievers Index, which trades over Amex with the symbol ^DAA. As of mid-2005, the index contained 313 stocks with a record of increasing dividends over 10 years or more.

Valuable Resource

Visit the Mergent Dividend Achievers website at http://finance.yahoo.com/q?s=%5EDAA.

Key Point

Companies that consistently raise their dividend are, by definition, well managed. Dividend history is one of the best ways to narrow down a list of potential investments.

This index, like other index investments, is appropriate for anyone who wants to diversify capital over many stocks. Of course, index returns tend to be averaged, notably when over 300 different stocks are involved. The Mergent index was initiated in 2003, so there is no long-term record of returns; but the selection criteria make the index a good match for many investors.

In picking individual stocks, dividend yield is a worthwhile means for comparison. For example, you may decide to limit your search for stocks based on dividend yield and, before applying other fundamental indicators, develop a short list of high-yielding companies. This is a method for picking well-managed companies; for example, you may decide to look only at stocks currently yielding 4 percent or more. Such a list would include some well-known companies such as Altria, ConAgra Foods, Consolidated Edison, National Fuel Gas Co., SBC Communications, United Mobile Homes, Washington Mutual, and numerous national and regional real estate holding companies and financial institutions.

An analysis of the popular fundamental indicators for these corporations reveals consistent revenue and earnings growth, strong capitalization, and consistently low price volatility. There are many other companies that offer strong fundamentals, albeit measured differently, and limiting your selection to high-ranked dividend achievers is no guarantee. Still it is a selection method that (1) shortens the list, (2) tends to focus on strong financial corporations, and (3) reduces market risk as experienced through low technical and fundamental volatility.

Studying Market Sectors

Another way to select corporations is by market sector. At any given time, some sectors are strong and others are weak. This relative strength or weakness can be measured in technical terms, specifically by way of price performance for sector stocks as a whole or by a combination of technical and fundamental attributes, including sensitivity to interest rates, dominance of unions in the labor force, or special problems and challenges. The airline industry has been troubled in recent years due to a combination of factors. These include rising fuel costs, international route competition, pressure from a high level of union employees for better wages and benefits, and problems with unrecorded pension liabilities. Several bankruptcies have defined the transportation sector in recent years, and a transition away from a competitive industry and toward a very limited number of carriers appears to be in the works.

Other factors affecting sectors are weak economic trends and high interest rates. The large retail sector, for example, experiences varying levels of consumer volume based on uncertainty about the economy, high or chronic unemployment, and even political unrest. The pharmaceutical industry faces significant exposure to lawsuits, as witnessed by the recent rash of lawsuits against Merck; even with FDA approval of specific drugs, companies in this sector are vulnerable to later discoveries of side effects.

While economic and political factors are major causes of sector weakness, they should not serve as the sole means for picking corporations or for rejecting sectors completely. These outside influences are among many possible causes for long-term buying opportunities or weakening growth prospects, depending on emerging news, cyclical change, political and global trends, and marketwide movements. On the technical side, some industries tend to follow the broader market closely, while other industries tend to be less responsive to index movements in stock values. An overall attitude of optimism or pessimism certainly affects stock prices, but for the fundamental analyst, dependence on hard facts and financial strength are invariably more dependable for forecasting the future.

Tax Policy and Stock Values

The ongoing national debate about tax policy has intensified in recent years, especially over the subject of investments. How should dividends be taxed? What rate should apply to long-term capital gains? Some people believe that investment income should be entirely exempt from federal income tax, arguing that such a change would add great strength to the market. While that may be true, the political cost of favoring investment returns could be substantial.

Key Point

Tax planning affects profitability as much as good selection and timing. Because the rules concerning investment income vary over time, tax liabilities are an important fundamental consideration in portfolio management.

Stock values reflect tax policy, to a degree. A review of year-round stock activity demonstrates that investors may time losses to reduce their taxable income in the current year or push gains forward to the future. Because the maximum deduction for net capital losses is limited to $3,000 per year, larger net losses can be absorbed by timing gains on other positions. A large carryover loss can be used to shelter current-year profits in this way.

Even without any changes in current tax rules, investors can time their buying and selling activity to reduce tax liabilities on their investments. A combined program including stocks as well as debt instruments and real estate may provide attractive tax reduction opportunities. Real estate investors can deduct up to $25,000 per year in operating losses (subject to some income limitations), which affects tax planning for stock portfolios as well. Investors with several rental properties may view a $25,000 new loss as tax shelter for stock portfolio gains in the same year.

State income tax rules further affect tax planning. Each state has its own rules, and these are often inconsistent with how income is treated for federal income tax purposes. You need to review both federal and state tax rules as part of a comprehensive tax planning strategy; this becomes especially crucial in years when you anticipate larger than average capital gains, dividend income, and interest income.

Valuable Resource

For a summary of income tax rules for each state, check http://www.taxadmin.org/fta/rate/ind_inc.html.

In cases where you reinvest your earnings, tax planning may involve cash flow planning as well. Because your earnings go back into the investment, you will not have cash available to pay your tax liabilities. This occurs when you own mutual fund shares and instruct the company to reinvest all earnings (dividends, interest, and capital gains). The tax liability on income remains, even though you do not take out any cash. A similar event occurs if you buy stocks and use dividend reinvestment plans (DRIPs) offered by the company (see Chapter 4).

Key Point

You can achieve compound returns on dividends even when you own stocks directly. The most efficient way is to use corporate DRIPs plans, which are explained in Chapter 4.

Valuable Resource

For direct links to corporations offering DRIPs programs, check http://www.wall-street.com/directlist.html.

Finding Information beyond the Statements

In the Internet age, your problem should not be a lack of information; if anything, the greater problem will be determining which information is valid and useful. There is so much free information available, it is difficult to distinguish junk from quality.

Fundamental analysis based on annual reports is easily obtained directly from corporations via their own websites. You can get to corporate websites from your brokerage website in most instances or through any site offering free quotes and charts. Doing a basic search on Google and other search engines invariably takes you to the corporate home page. From there, look for a link—or perform a search on "Investor Relations" or "Annual Reports"—and you will find the source material you want. This usually includes archives of partial reports.

If you want hard copy, you can telephone the corporation and ask for a copy of the annual report directly, to be sent by mail. All listed companies will provide you with free annual reports and quarterly updates. Good sources for immediate contact by Internet or mail include the stock exchanges themselves, which list and link to all member corporations shown in Table 11.1. These are excellent sources for beginning your investigation of a company's financial statements. Even with ready access to financial information, however, it is surprising that investments decisions are often made impulsively, based on technical trends (specifically, price movement) or even gossip and rumor.

TABLE 11.1   Stock Exchanges

New York Stock Exchange—http://www.nyse.com

11 Wall Street, New York NY 10005

Phone: 212-656-3000

Link: *Listed company directory*

NASDAQ—http://www.nasdaq.com

165 Broadway, New York NY 10006

Phone: 212-401-8700

Link: *Investor Tools: Annual Reports, Listed Companies: National Market List*

American Stock Exchange—http://www.amex.com

86 Trinity Place, New York NY 10006

Phone: 212-306-1000

Link: (Open all menus link) *Listed Companies*

Philadelphia Stock Exchange—http://www.phlx.com

1900 Market Street, Philadelphia PA 19103

Phone: 1-800-843-7459 or 1-215-496-5000

No link was found on the website for member companies. A "quick link" can be used to enter a trading symbol to be directed to a specific company—or a search can be performed on a broader search engine.

Analysis in its different forms is merely a way to facilitate good decisions. There are no sure-fire systems, no way to beat the market, and no risk-free investments. The purpose of analysis is to improve the *rate* of profitable decisions over unprofitable ones.

Key Point
Factual analysis provides you better data for making good decisions, to improve your rate of profits over losses.

A widespread belief—akin to wishful thinking—is that analysis may help you to ensure profits consistently, beat the market, and "get rich quick." As it turns out, the uncertainties of market price movement even over the long term make this an unrealistic goal. In the rest of this chapter you will see how many investors operate on the concept of beating the market, and unintentionally move from fundamentally based decisions to technically based ones. While technical indicators are useful in the overall process of making decisions, a fundamental investor also needs to ensure that the basis on which decisions are made conforms to the self-definition every investor holds. Are you going to depend on the fundamentals? If so, you need to ensure that you do not find yourself reacting to short-term technical change as a primary means for buying and selling.

Buy Low, Sell High

The best example of technical information is price. A stock's current market price is easily accessible, it changes frequently, and it dominates the news. Television financial programs summarize each day's leading rising and falling stocks (usually based on number of points rather than percentage of change), which is misleading as well as incidental. What is really going on? It would make more sense to report stocks in terms of earnings, current yield, or P/E.

For example, let's say that on today's news the following leading rising stocks are reported:

Stock A	up 3 points at $27
Stock B	up 4 points at $52
Stock C	up 5 points at $80

The way financial news is reported—with emphasis on the number of points involved—it would appear that Stock C had the best record today. Yet when you add in the *percentage* increase from the previous day's close, you get a different picture:

Stock A	up 3 points at $27, or 12.5%
Stock B	up 4 points at $52, or 8.3%
Stock C	up 5 points at $80, or 6.7%

The above case illustrates why points are meaningless. The three-point gain of Stock A is nearly twice the gain of Stock C. So on a dollar-for-dollar basis, if you owned 300 shares of Stock A, your investment level would be approximately the same as owning 100 shares of Stock C; but your one-day gain would have been far better.

The way that financial news is reported is inaccurate and off the point. Emphasis on daily price change is precisely the kind of information most investors should ignore. Only day traders and other speculators should really be interested in short-term price change; most fundamental investors are more interested in different questions:

- Do the fundamentals continue to support this company as a long-term growth investment?

- Have any important fundamental trends changed (e.g., dividend, revenue and earnings, P/E ratio)?

- What major changes or developments are occurring that may affect this company's ongoing competitive position?

These all-important questions are more important but less interesting in a financial journalism environment, where sound bites have to grab and hold attention, but only briefly. Thus, if you get your primary financial news from television programs, you are not likely to find out what you need to know.

The rather pat advice these shows normally provide are formula based. They are designed to draw in audiences based on promises to tell you which stocks are hot right now. The price is low, so you should buy. When the price is higher, you should sell. This "buy low, sell high" advice is common and trite and, more to the point, it leaves off the much more important second half: Buy low, sell high . . . *instead of the other way around.*

Key Point

Good advice tells you to buy low and sell high . . . instead of the other way around.

Investors struggle continuously with the double problems typical whenever money is at stake: greed and panic. These emotional incentives make it far more likely to buy high and sell low. When you consider the ramifications of this, it becomes apparent that many investors do, indeed, make their decisions backwards, which also explains why it is so common to time decisions poorly and to lose money.

Greed operates at and near market tops. When a stock begins a fast rise in price, more investors tend to get in at the top than anywhere else. When the stock exhausts its run-up, those investors are stuck with overpriced shares. One way to estimate a market top is to watch buy volume; a price rise is likely to be near the exhaustion point when that volume increases.

Panic operates at the bottom. The same investors who try to cash in on a rising stock by buying shares at market tops also tend to panic when prices fall; they are likely to sell at or near the bottom price. When sell volume is maximized, that often signals a buying opportunity.

Resisting greed and panic is difficult, because they are the human tendencies. Doing the opposite—following the contrarian principle—is difficult to follow in practice. It is natural to want to cash in when you see prices rises, and to cut losses when prices are falling. Generally speaking, however, the calmer, long-term growth investor, who follows the fundamentals and ignores short-term price trends, is likely to make higher profits and suffer fewer losses over time.

There is a saying, "Bulls and bears can make money in the market, but pigs and chickens cannot." Fundamental analysis provides you with the keys for identifying and interpreting concrete, important financial facts and for making smart decisions based on what those facts reveal. You may equate fundamental analysis with science because it is based on factual and long-term information rather than on short-term price changes. For most people, the long term is far more important. The question is not whether you will turn a profit by next week, but whether your capital will be intact in the next decade.

Glossary

How often misused words generate misleading thoughts.
—Herbert Spencer, *Principles of Ethics*, 1892–1893

accounts payable   a current liability reflecting all of the currently owed costs and expenses; the account is used to recognize costs and expenses in a current period even though they will not be paid until later.

accounts receivable   a current asset consisting of balances due from customers, used to report earned income in the proper accounting period even when cash will not be received until later.

accrual   a system in accounting of booking revenues, costs, and expenses prior to cash exchanging hands; the purpose is to book these in the proper accounting period. It often occurs that cash transacts later than the period income is earned or expenses are incurred.

accrued expenses   those expenses that are payable but not yet paid, representing currently incurred obligations that will be billed by invoice or statement in the future, usually in the following month.

accumulated depreciation   the value of all depreciation claimed on fixed assets from the date of purchase through the latest balance sheet date. Long-term assets are reported at purchase price minus accumulated depreciation and remain on the balance sheet until those assets are sold. Eventually, fully depreciated assets will report a net value of zero—once the full purchase price has been completely depreciated. At that point, the accumulated depreciation will be equal to the purchase price of the asset.

acid test   a ratio similar to the current ratio, but excluding inventory. The general standard for an "acceptable" acid test is 1 to 1 between current assets (without inventory) and current liabilities. Also called *quick assets ratio*.

amortization   writing down an account over a period of time—such as when a prepaid asset is gradually amortized so that the expense is reported in the applicable month and year.

annual report   a publication released by listed companies to disclose to stockholders and regulators all of the relevant information about the company and its operations: markets and products, financial statements with footnotes, and summaries from the executive management of the company.

asset allocation a strategic portfolio management technique for identifying how capital should be divided among major markets (usually stocks, bonds, and real estate), based on current market and economic conditions, risk tolerance, and individual investment goals.

assets the properties owned by a company, listed on the balance sheet in dollar value and making up the first of three sections on the balance sheet.

bad debts accounts receivable carried on the corporate books as a current asset that will become uncollectible in the future. A reserve is set up to estimate bad debts likely to occur based on receivables booked each year.

balance sheet one of three financial statements, reporting values of assets, liabilities, and net worth as of a specific date; that date is the ending date of a quarter or year. The total of assets (properties) is equal to the sum of liabilities (debts) and net worth (equity of the company).

balance sheet ratios those ratios comparing account balances found on a corporation's balance sheet (1) at the end of a period or (2) between years or quarters.

bar chart a form of price charting in which a series of daily prices is shown side by side over time. The vertical bar shows the range of prices during the day from high to low. A small horizontal extension to the right shows the closing price for the day and some bar charts also include a small horizontal extension to the left for the day's opening price.

beta a technical test of a stock's volatility in comparison to the market as a whole. The degree to which a stock's price historically tracks larger market price movement determines its beta.

bonds for corporations, long-term debts payable with interest to debt investors; for investors, an alternative form of investment including a promise for repayment of principal as well as periodic payments of a stated and fixed rate of interest.

book value per share the value of a company, expressed on a per-share basis. The net worth is divided by the average shares issued and outstanding during the year, and the result is expressed in dollars and cents per share.

bottom line the last value on the income statement, representing the earnings after all operating costs and expenses, interest, and taxes have been deducted from revenues.

breakaway gap a sudden movement in a stock's price involving space between past and current trading range *and* also above or below the established trading range.

breakeven calculation a formula used to determine the required breakeven point for investments, considering the effects of both inflation and income taxes. To calculate, divide the current inflation rate by the rate of after-tax income. (After-tax income is 100 minus an individual's tax rate, including both federal and state.)

breakout a price movement above resistance or below support levels, which signals a change in trading range and volatility for a stock.

candlestick chart a form of chart that efficiently summarizes a day's trading range, high and low price, and direction of movement.

capital assets   expenditures that are required by tax law to be capitalized (reported as assets on the balance sheet) rather than written off as current-year expenses in the year purchased. These are reported at net value (purchase price minus accumulated depreciation).

capital stock   the reported issue value of all outstanding stock at original value, shown as the first item in a corporation's net worth section of the balance sheet.

capitalization   (1) the equity value of a company, also known as *market capitalization* or *market cap*; it is computed by multiplying total issued shares of common stock by the current price per share; (2) the total debt and equity of a corporation; the combination of net worth and long-term debt.

cash flow   the trail of funds moving in and out of the organization, which can be tracked and watched as a means for determining fiscal health. Cash flow management determines how effectively an organization is able to fund current and future operating demands and growth.

Certified Financial Planner (CFP)   a professional designation awarded to individuals who hold a BA degree, complete an education program, pass a 10-hour exam, and complete three years of experience in the field.

chart   the basic tool of technical analysis, used to study price movements in the belief that specific patterns signal how future prices will change.

close-only chart   a price tracking chart showing closing price only, but not the range of high and low price ranges.

common gap   chart pattern involving a space between the previous trading range and a new opening price; an insignificant adjustment in a stock's price range.

comparative statement   a financial statement that summarizes results from year to year, between the same quarter-ending of subsequent years, or in some other breakdown such as between divisions and operating units of a larger corporation.

confirmation   the principle that a second indicator must move in the same direction as the primary indicator to establish a new trend; and that both indicators need to reverse direction before another change in trend is identified.

consolidated statement   a type of financial statement including combined results from all subsidiaries, even those in dissimilar lines of business.

contingent liability   a potential obligation that may or may not become an actual liability in the future, such as pending lawsuits filed against the company.

contrarian investing   a tendency among better-informed investors to anticipate coming trends and to trade accordingly—buying bargain-priced stocks when others are selling, and selling overpriced stocks when others continue to buy.

cookie jar accounting   the practice of moving profits from an exceptionally high-profit year to a future relatively low-profit year in order to even out the reported revenues and profits. Also called *sugar bowl accounting*.

core earnings   the revenues and profits a corporation earns during the year from its primary business activity, and excluding nonrecurring revenues.

core net worth   the net worth of a corporation reflecting the accurate and total value of all assets and liabilities, including unrecorded or inaccurately recorded items.

core P/E ratio   the price/earnings ratio using the adjusted core earnings in place of reported net earnings (or net income) used in the traditional P/E calculation.

cost accounting   a type of accounting focusing on detailed analysis and study of manufacturing costs for the purpose of identifying inefficiencies and controlling unit costs of production.

cost of goods sold   the section on the statement of operations following reported revenues. Cost of goods sold consists of changes in inventory levels; merchandise purchased; direct labor; and other costs attributable directly to generating revenues. The cost of goods sold is deducted from sales to arrive at gross profit.

credit   a right-sided entry and part of equal debits and credits in all instances as part of a double-entry bookkeeping system; the purpose of debits and credits is to ensure that the books are always in balance.

current assets   those assets in the form of cash or that are convertible to cash within 12 months, including accounts and notes receivable, marketable securities, and inventory.

current liabilities   all of the debts of a company that are payable within the next 12 months, including accounts and taxes payable, lease payments, and payments on loans and notes.

current ratio   a test of working capital, computed by dividing current assets by current liabilities. The result is expressed in the form of x to y and the general standard for an acceptable current ratio level is 2 to 1 or better.

current yield   the percentage return investors earn from dividends paid by a corporation. To calculate, divide the full year's dividend payment by the current stock price. As the stock price falls, current yield rises; and as the stock price rises, current yield declines.

debit   a left-sided entry and part of equal debits and credits in all instances as part of a double-entry bookkeeping system; the purpose of debits and credits is to ensure that the books are always in balance.

debt   the value of liabilities of a corporation; to an investor, the value of bonds owned. Bond investors receive compensation by way of interest, as well as discounted value of the bond based on interest rates paid versus current market rates.

debt ratio   the portion of total capitalization represented by debt, as opposed to equity sources; when debt levels rise and corporations become less able to continue dividend payments or fund future operations.

debt-equity ratio   alternate name for the debt ratio; a ratio demonstrating relationships between debt and equity capitalization.

deferred assets   the value of costs and expenses paid currently but applying to a future period. Those payments are deferred so that they can be booked as costs or expenses in the future. In the following year or years, the deferred asset is reduced and the applicable amount transferred to the income statement.

deferred credits sales and other credits received in advance of the applicable reporting period, recorded in the liability section of the balance sheet pending transfer in the future to the operating statement.

deferred income any income received in the current period but not earned until a future period; this is properly set up as a deferred credit in the liability section of the balance sheet, to be reversed later when the revenue becomes earned (for example, when goods are shipped to the customer).

depreciation a noncash expense reflecting periodic value of capital assets. All capital assets (except land) are fully depreciated over a period of years, involving regular annual allowances (straight-line depreciation) or larger write-offs in the earlier years and lower write-offs later (accelerated depreciation). All capital assets except land are depreciated over several years.

diversification risk the risk that a portfolio will not be invested in enough different issues, markets, or venues to ensure safety; a nondiversified portfolio is subject to the same cyclical or economic forces, which places the entire portfolio at greater risk.

dividend reinvestment programs (DRIPs) services provided by many corporations allowing stockholders to take dividends in additional partial shares instead of cash dividends. For example, if current share price is $75 per share and the quarterly dividend is $25, a DRIPs plan would allow the stockholder to acquire an additional one-third share.

double-entry bookkeeping the system of entering transactions in the books and records of a company, whether consisting of cash or accruals; all entries consist of a left-sided debit and a right-sided credit. The two sides always contain equal value, so that the control feature is designed to guarantee mathematical accuracy. The sum of all debits and all credits should always be zero.

Dow Theory a technical market theory based on the writings of Charles Dow. The theory is based on a belief that primary movements in stock indices establish and confirm marketwide trends.

earned income revenues earned in one period and properly reported in that period even if actual payment will not occur until later; to report income accurately, earned income is entered by way of a journal entry, offset by an addition to the current asset, accounts receivable.

earnings announcements published summaries of quarterly earnings per share that a publicly traded corporation reports to the SEC. The announcement is used on Wall Street in comparison to analysts' earnings estimates.

earnings per share (EPS) an important fundamental indicator, reflecting net earnings each year per outstanding share. The earnings are divided by the shares outstanding to arrive at the EPS, which is reported in dollars and cents.

efficient market theory a belief about the market, stating that the current price of stock reflects all known information at any given time; the concept that pricing of stocks is efficient because it is based on the collective knowledge of the market.

equity   the value of ownership; in a listed corporation, equity consists of all classes of stock plus retained earnings. Equity investors are compensated by way of dividends and long-term capital gains.

exchange traded funds   types of mutual funds with a preidentified basket of stocks in its portfolio and whose shares trade over public exchanges just like individual stocks.

exhaustion gap   the conclusion of a period of strong price movement, in which the gap pattern precedes a reversal in the gap-specific price change. The exhaustion gap is recognizable only in hindsight.

expenses   the grouping of spending reported on the statement of operations, for obligations not directly tied to generation of revenues. These include both selling expenses and general and administrative expenses and are the focus of internal controls, especially during periods of rapid sales expansion.

exponential moving average   a type of weighted moving average, the formula for which gives greater weight to the most recent field value, while accumulating the overall average by adding the latest value to the existing field.

financial planner   an individual with experience and credentials to advise investors on how to pick stocks and other products. A qualified planner should hold the CFP designation.

fiscal year   the corporate 12-month period used for closing the books and reporting taxes as well as annual financial statements. A fiscal year does not always correspond to a calendar year, but may end on any month of the corporation's choosing, often set based on natural market and economic cycles.

flags   short-term trading patterns in a specific direction in which the gap between high and low remains constant.

footnotes   a series of explanatory notes, often including detailed narrative and financial breakdowns, to disclose important information and to expand upon the summarized data provided in the financial statements. Footnotes exist for dozens of purposes and are included as part of a complete set of financial statements.

front-end load   an accounting term referring to the practice of recognizing revenues too early; a deceptive accounting decision to inflate current earnings by overstating revenues.

fundamental analysis   the study of a company's financial strength, based on historical data; sector and industry position; management; dividend history; capitalization; and the potential for future growth. The combination of historical information and fiscal status collectively represent all data not directly related to the price of stock, and this body of information is used to define value investing and to compare one stock to another.

fundamental volatility   the degree of change from one year to the next in reported sales, costs, expenses, and earnings, as well as inconsistency in other fundamental trends, dividend payments, and ratio tests.

gaps   spaces between one day's close and another day's opening price.

generally accepted accounting principles (GAAP)   a series of rules, opinions, and guidelines governing accounting and auditing practices and used within the industry to regulate the decisions and activities of independent auditors.

gross margin   the percentage of gross profit to revenues on the income statement.

gross profit   the net difference between revenues and direct costs, or profit before expenses. It is a line item on the statement of operations following direct costs and preceding general and administrative expenses.

head and shoulders   a price trend pattern involving three stages. In an upward head and shoulders pattern, stages one and three show prices reaching a resistance level before retreating, and the middle stage tracking the same movements but with a higher resistance level. In a downward head and shoulders pattern, the same stages exist, but they involve support levels rather than resistance.

income statement ratios   tests of financial trends and status based on comparisons between accounts found on the income statement, or outcomes found on income statements and tracked over a period of time.

inflation risk   the risk that investment net yield will be lower than inflation. Consequently, your portfolio loses value when purchasing power (after-inflation value) is taken in to account.

intangible assets   the recorded value of assets that have no physical existence, such as goodwill or incomplete agreements. These are recorded along with other assets, but these would be excluded from the calculation of *tangible* book value of a company.

inventory turnover   a test of management's efficiency in keeping inventory levels at the right general range. High turnover indicates that inadequate supplies are held, and a trend toward lower rates of turnover indicates poor use of working capital or stocking of slow-moving goods.

investment club   an informal organization of individuals who meet to share research chores, pool their money, and identify profitable investments; funds contributed by members are invested as a unit in the investments selected through the club members' research.

issued shares   common stock of a listed corporation available for public trading, including closely held shares owned by directors, officers, and founding family members, and the value of shares that may be issued in the future to honor outstanding stock options.

journal entries   adjustments made to the books and records to correct errors, report transactions that belong in the current period but that have not yet occurred, to move transactions to later periods when they occur too soon, and to record noncash transactions.

lease commitments   liabilities under contract, often long-term, to pay rent for equipment, rights, or real estate. These liabilities are probably not recorded on the financial statement of a corporation and can only be found in the footnotes.

liquidity   an attribute of an asset relating to its convertibility to cash. Some assets can be quickly and easily converted to cash and are considered highly liquid; other assets cannot be easily or quickly converted, and those assets have low liquidity.

liquidity risk (investment funds) the risk that funds may not be readily available in particular markets, which have high liquidity risk, versus other markets in which funds can be converted to cash very quickly, which contain low liquidity risk; (markets) the risk that buyers and sellers may not be easily matched. For example, in a slow real estate market, there will be more sellers than buyers so properties may not sell for the currently asked price; in the stock market, specialists ensure an orderly market by completing orders even when buyers and sellers are not matched.

long-term assets also called "fixed" assets, are the purchased value of assets that cannot be deducted in the year purchased but must be depreciated over time. On the balance sheet, long-term assets are reported at purchase price minus accumulated depreciation.

long-term liabilities all debts of a company extended beyond the next 12 months, including payments on contracts, notes and loans; bonds; and other liabilities not due within the coming 12 months.

long-term notes payable debts of a corporation that are payable beyond the next 12 months, including intermediate-term loans, mortgages, and long-term obligations.

lost opportunity risk the risk that, due to the way investment capital is committed, other profit opportunities will be lost. The most common example involves buying stocks that remain at a set price, while other stocks rise in value.

margin a gap, remainder, or space between groupings of accounts on the income statement, usually expressed as a percentage; at times interchangeable with "return" and "yield." Typically, analysts study gross margin, operating margin, and pretax margin.

market capitalization the market value of all common stock issued and outstanding, computed by multiplying total common shares by the current market price per share.

market risk the risk that an investment's market value will fall or that stocks are purchased at the wrong time, so that a temporary downward price movement results in a paper loss that may take time to recover.

moving average a statistical tool used by market analysts, involving the use of a field of values over time. The moving average employs a specific number of field values and as a new value is added, an older one is dropped off.

multiple in the P/E ratio, the outcome; the number of times current earnings are reflected in the price per share of stock.

net operating profit or loss the net remaining when expenses are deducted from gross profit, representing profit or loss from operations but excluding nonoperating income or expenses.

net profit or loss the net sum of operating profit or loss adjusted for other income and expense. It is the reported net amount that will be added to or subtracted from retained earnings and carried forward on the permanent books of the corporation.

net return the return on sales, usually expressed as a percentage. Earnings are divided by revenues to determine the net return.

net worth the value of a corporation; the difference between assets and liabilities, consisting of capital stock, retained earnings, current profit or loss; and minus obligation for dividend payments.

nonrecurring gains   any gain from the sale of capital assets, reclassified balance sheet accounts, or other adjustments that may distort the financial picture unless they are removed from the trend analysis.

off-balance sheet transaction   any transaction of a company not shown on the balance sheet or operating statement. These include lease obligations, contingent liabilities, and unconsolidated subsidiary company operating results.

operating profit   the profit after costs and expenses are deducted from revenues but not counting "other" income and expenses such as interest, capital gains and losses, or currency exchange, and also not counting liability for income taxes.

other income or expense   the adjustments made to operating profit or loss for non-operating items, including currency exchange, interest income and expense, and income tax liabilities. The operating profit or loss is adjusted for the net difference, resulting in overall net profit.

P/B ratio   price to book value per share, based on the calculation of tangible assets rather than on all assets. Price is divided by tangible net worth (net worth minus intangible assets) to arrive at the ratio, which is expressed as a numeric value.

P/C ratio   a comparison between a stock's current price and the company's ending balance of cash per share. This may include only cash, or the combination of cash and short-term investments in marketable securities.

P/S ratio   the ratio of price per share, to sales (revenue) per share. The equation normally uses a full year's revenues per share, and is most accurate when tracked over many years.

pennants   short-term trading patterns in a specific direction in which the gap between high and low converges over time.

pension liabilities   the amount of money due to retired employees and accumulating in the accounts of current employees and due in the future. Pension liabilities are often substantial, but are normally not recorded on the balance sheet and can be found only in the footnotes to the financial statements.

percentage of completion (POC)   a method of accounting in which revenues are recognized periodically based on the degree of job completion; used by construction and similar industries, POC is an estimate intended to recognize earnings during a lengthy process.

point-and-figure chart   a type of chart used by technicians to track price but not time. Rising prices and trends are represented by a series of Xs and the stronger the movement, the more Xs appear. Downward prices and trends are shown as a series of vertical Os.

portfolio management   a series of tests and monitoring procedures designed to ensure that a stock's fundamental strength remains; when that position changes, it may also be time to sell the stock.

prepaid assets   the net value of expenses paid this year when all or part applies to the future. In the applicable period, a portion of the prepaid asset is reduced and recorded as an expense, so that it is recognized in the correct reporting year.

prepaid expenses   those expenses paid in advance and set up as prepaid assets to be amortized over a period of months; the result is to reflect the expense in the proper periods.

pretax profit   the net profit after all costs and expenses are deducted from revenues, before deducting liability for federal, state, or local income taxes.

price trends   the tendencies of stock prices to behave in particular ways over time, and to demonstrate patterns that, in the view of the technical analyst, reveal how prices are going to move next.

price/earnings ratio (PE ratio)   an important ratio comparing the current price per share to the latest known *earnings per share* (EPS). The PE multiple summarizes the market's perception about the number of times' earnings the stock should be worth, and it is a combination of both technical (price) and fundamental (earnings) information.

profit or loss   the net reported annual profits earned by a corporation. The reported net profit or loss on the operating statement also appears as a single item on the net worth section of the corporation's balance sheet and, upon closing the books for the year, net profit or loss is added to the accumulated retained earnings.

quick assets ratio   a variation of the current ratio, also called the *acid test*. The general standard for an acceptable quick assets ratio is 1 to 1 between current assets (without inventory) and current liabilities.

random walk hypothesis   a theory concerning the stock market that all price movement is random because it results from a range of supply and demand causes.

ratio   an analytical expression of relationships between values, expressed in fractional or percentage form. The ratio clarifies numerical relationships and makes trend analysis easier to manage and understand.

recognition   in accounting the process of booking revenues and costs and expenses in the proper period, even when cash has not yet traded hands. The purpose of recognizing items early is to make the reported books accurate in order to include not only cash but earned income and incurred costs and expenses.

reserve for bad debts   an account shown in the current assets section of the balance sheet reducing accounts receivable. It represents an estimate of future bad debts based on current accounts receivable levels.

resistance   the highest likely price for a stock within its established trading range.

retained earnings   the accumulated net profits or losses a company has reported over its history; profits are added and losses are subtracted, from the previous year's net retained earnings.

return   the profit remaining when costs and expenses are deducted from revenues; the percentage of profits on original amount invested; or the percentage of profits to equity in a corporation—various types of calculations, usually expressed as a percentage, in analysis of the income statement.

return on equity   a ratio comparing profits before interest and taxes (operating profit) to a corporation's net worth.

revenues   (also called *sales*) gross earnings of a corporation before costs and expenses; the first line on the statement of operations.

risk tolerance   the level of risk appropriate to each individual investor, based on income, assets, knowledge, and experience; the amount of market risk and other forms of risk a person is able and willing to tolerate.

runaway gap   an extreme price gap pattern in which a series of recurring gaps moving above or below previously established trading range signals an important change in the stock's trading levels.

Sarbanes-Oxley Act (SOX)   a 2002 federal law regulating accountants, executives, and securities analysts in reporting to the public and in disclosing potential conflicts of interest; and established to increase regulatory funding to investigate corporate practices by the Securities and Exchange Commission (SEC).

Shareholder Relations Department   a department within a publicly listed corporation set up specifically to address concerns and answer questions from shareholders. A test of corporate transparency and investor services is to test this department's response to financial questions.

shareholders' equity   (also called *stockholders' equity*) the net worth of a company, consisting of several accounts but essentially the net remaining after liabilities are subtracted from assets.

simple moving average   the most basic variation of the moving average. A field of the most recent values is averaged and, as each new value is entered, the oldest value is dropped off so that the number of values studied remains constant.

specialist   an individual working in a stock exchange whose function is to ensure an orderly market, completing orders even when buyers and sellers are not equal.

spikes   exceptionally big changes in price, upward or downward, when compared to established trading levels; and characterized by a return to previous levels after the spike.

statement of cash flows   the financial statement used to summarize the movement of cash in and out of a business over a period of time, also called the cash flow statement or statement of sources and applications of funds.

statement of operations   (also called *income statement* or *profit and loss statement*) the financial statement summarizing activity for a specific period of time, usually a quarter or fiscal year. The major sections of the statement are revenues, costs, expenses, and profits.

sugar bowl accounting   movement of reported totals from high-profit years to future low-profit years in order to even out reported operating results. Also called *cookie jar accounting*

support   the lowest likely price for a stock within its established trading range.

tangible book value per share   the book value per share, excluding all intangible assets. This is an adjustment to book value per share, in which intangible assets are subtracted from total net worth.

tax risk   the exposure of investments to tax liabilities. Investment yield and risk should be evaluated on an after-tax basis to allow for the tax risk in the equation.

technical analysis   a series of techniques employed to anticipate price movement in stocks; to study the causes and patterns of price and volume; and to anticipate the direction price is likely to move in the near future. Unlike fundamental analysis, which is rooted in financial reports of the corporation, technical analysis is primarily involved in prices and trends of a company's stock.

total capitalization   the combination of long-term debt and shareholders' equity; the source of financing to fund corporate operations, consisting of debt and equity capital.

trading range   the distance between a stock's established high and low prices over a period of time, representing the current levels of price supply and demand for the stock.

transparency   a concept in corporate management defining the desirability of making full disclosures to stockholders so that operations, financial results, and accounting decisions are made in the open; the idea that nothing should be hidden from the investor or stockholder.

trend   a long-term tendency reflected in how a corporation's financial results change over time; how related accounts emerge as status changes; and how a previously established pattern of growth begins, often gradually, to change.

triangles   trading patterns in which the range of high-to-low prices broadens or narrows within a short period of time.

V formations   a price pattern typified by a sharp increase or decrease in price to a new high or low level, followed immediately by a sharp reversal and price movement in the opposite direction.

valuable resource   for more information about the DJIA, component stocks, weighting, and other links, check the Dow Jones website at http://averages.dowjones.com.

volatility   the tendency of stock prices to change or move in a trading range over time. High volatility is characterized by a broad trading range and widely varying price trends; low volatility is characterized by a narrow trading range and stable price trends.

weighted moving average   a variation of moving average in which greater influence is given to more recent field values and less to older field values.

working capital   the funds available to a corporation to fund ongoing operations for the immediate future, and a test applied to test and compare cash flow. Working capital is the net difference between current assets and current liabilities.

write-off   the process of reducing an asset's value and converting it to an expense. This occurs when an asset becomes valueless or, in the case of capital assets, through recording of periodic depreciation.

yield   the return, profit, and percentage gained. The term is used on the income statement to compare profits to revenues, amount invested, or equity; or to compare dividends to the current stock price.

Notes

Chapter 3

1. John A. Byrne, "Joe Berardino's Fall from Grace," *Business Week*, 12 August 2002.
2. Financial Accounting Standards Board "FASB Facts," *FASB.org* <http://www.fasb.org/facts> (28 October 2005).
3. Harvey Pitt, "Regulation of the Accounting Profession," 17 January 2002.
4. Staff, "New York's Bubble Boys" and "How Spitzer Pact Will Affect Wall Street" *Wall Street Journal*, 22 May 2002.
5. Staff, "Should You Trust Wall Street's New Ratings?" *Wall Street Journal*, 17 July 2002.
6. Mary Williams Walsh, "G.M. Tops List as Study Questions Pension Accounting," *New York Times*, 30 June 2005.

Chapter 4

1. Howard Schilit, *Financial Shenanigans* (New York: McGraw-Hill, 2002), 12.

Index

ABCs of Stock Speculation, 43
Accounting methods, 92
Accounts payable, 98–99
Accounts receivable, 98, 101, 147, 161–162
Accruals, 96–97
Accumulated depreciation, 17
Acid test, 143
Adelphia, 57
Affiliate, 158
Altria Corporation, 63–64, 106–107, 131, 206
American Institute of Certified Public
    Accountants (AICPA), 61
American Stock Exchange (AMEX), 79, 210
Amortization, 102
Annual report, 78, 209
AOL, 112
Applications of funds, 24
Arthur Andersen, 57, 58–59, 88
Asset allocation, 52
Assets, 15–16
AT&T, 111
Audit conduct, 58–60, 70–71

Bad debts, 101, 146–147, 161–162
Balance sheet
    assets, 15–16, 138
    comparative, 27–29
    explained, 14–18
    footnotes, 29–31
    inter-period analysis, 151–152
    liabilities, 16–17, 139
    net worth, 17–18, 139
    organization, 19
    ratios, 137–138
    unrecorded liabilities, 91, 113, 153–154
Bar chart, 35
Beta, 122
Blue Chips, 118
Book value per share, 182–183

Boston Chicken, 110–111
Bottom line, 156
Boyd's Collection, 167–169
Breakaway gap, 196
Breakeven calculation, 53–55
Breakout, 38, 196
Burger King, 166

Candlestick chart, 36–37
Capital assets, 16
Capitalization, 82, 147–151
Cash flow, 127–128
Certified Financial Planner (CFP), 89–90
Charles Schwab & Company, 195
Chubb, 131
Cineplex Odeon, 112
Cisco, 114, 116
Citigroup, 61, 177–180, 188
Close-only chart, 36
Colgate-Palmolive, 131
Combined analysis methods, 39–42, 190–195
Common gap, 196
Compaq Computers, 116
Comparative financial statements, 27–29
ConAgra Foods, 206
Confirmation, 44, 122–130, 195–199
Consolidated Edison, 206
Contingent liabilities, 91–92, 113
Contrarian investing, 44
Cookie jar accounting, 95
Core earnings adjustments, 71–75, 116–119,
    179–181
Core net worth, 118
Corporate scandals, 67–69, 104
Corporate websites, 78–80
Cost accounting, 184
Cost of goods sold, 20–21
Credit Suisse First Boston, 68
Current assets and liabilities, 139–140

Current ratio, 140–141
Current yield, 156, 204

Debt ratio, 82, 148–151
Deferred income, 100, 114
Deloitte & Touche, 57
Depreciation, 102
Diebold, 131
Diversification risk, 51, 165
Dividend Achievers, 81, 205–206
Dividend reinvestment programs (DRIPs), 81
Dividends declared, 81, 131, 193, 204–206
Double-entry bookkeeping, 99
Dow, Charles, 43
Dow Jones Corporation, 104
Dow Jones Industrial Averages (DJIA),
    42, 122–123, 194
Dow Theory, 42–45, 119, 122–124, 195

Earned income, 96–97
Earnings announcements, 87–88
Earnings per share (EPS), 82, 156–157,
    160–161, 174
Eastman Kodak, 83
Efficient market theory, 46–47
Eli Lilly, 131
Emerson Electric, 131
Enron, 57, 104, 106
Exchange traded funds (ETFs), 52
Exhaustion gap, 197
Expansion trends, 163–164, 165
Expense capitalization, 111–112
Expenses, 21
Exponential moving average, 10–11, 13–14
ExxonMobil, 79

Financial Accounting Standards Board
    (FASB), 60–61
Financial planner, 89
Financial Planning Association (FPA), 90
Financial statements, 5–8, 89–93
Fiscal year, 101
Flags, 39
Food and Drug Administration (FDA), 87, 207
Footnotes, 29–31, 62–64
Ford Motor Company, 73
Front-end load, 108
Fuller, 131
Fundamental theories, 8, 34–39, 130–132, 203
Fundamental volatility, 81, 105

GAAP system, 60–62, 71–74, 92, 96, 104,
    113–114, 119
Gannett, 131
Gaps, 39, 196–197
General Electric, 78, 110, 114
General Motors, 73, 118, 128, 199
Goldman Sachs, 68
Google, 79, 209
Gross margin, 156, 162
Gross profit, 21, 159

Hamilton, Peter, 43
Head and shoulders, 39
Heinz, 131
Hewlett-Packard, 83
Hong Kong GAAP, 74
Hormel, 131

IBM, 73, 78, 107, 111, 142–143, 166, 181
Inflation risk, 53
International Accounting Standards (IAS), 74
Internet, 209
Inventory turnover, 144, 162
Investment clubs, 90
Investor Relations, 157, 171, 209

JC Penney, 79, 170
Johnson & Johnson, 131
Jones, Edward C., 43
Journal entries, 97
JPMorgan Chase, 68

Key facts, 80–85
K-Mart, 164
KPMG, 57
Kraft Foods, 64

Lease commitments, 91
Lehman, 68
Liabilities, 16–17
Liquidity risk, 50
Lockheed, 112–113
Lost opportunity risk, 50

Magical thinking, 202
Margin, 156
Market capitalization, 147–148
Market risk, 50
Market sectors, 206

Market share, 164
Marsh & McLennan, 131
McGraw-Hill, 131
Medicare, 115
Merck, 207
Mergent Corporation, 81, 205
Mergers and acquisitions, 88, 165
Merrill Lynch, 67–68, 110
Microsoft, 107, 114, 115, 142–143, 181
Miller Brewing, 106–107
Morgan Stanley, 68
Motorola, 150–151
Moving averages, 7–14

NASDAQ, 44, 79, 122, 194, 210
National Association of Investors Corporation
     (NAIC), 90
National Association of Securities Dealers
     (NASD), 68
National Fuel Gas Company, 206
Nelson, Samuel, 43
Net profit, 21, 156, 160–161
Net worth, 17–18
New York Stock Exchange (NYSE), 79, 210
Noncash expenses, 102
Nonrecurring gains, 110

Off-balance sheet transactions, 66, 113
Operating profit, 157
Orion Pictures, 112
Other income and expense, 21

Pennants, 39
Pension liabilities, 91
PepsiCo, 131
P/E ratio
     calculation, 176
     core, 179–180
     defined, 82
     development, 174–178
     EPS and, 174–175
     multiple, 173–174
     outdated, 131
     trends, 132–134
Percentage of Completion (POC), 110
Pfizer, 131
Philadelphia Stock Exchange (PHLX), 210
Pitt, Harvey, 62
Point-and-figure chart, 36
Polaroid, 199

Portfolio management, 86
Prepaid expenses, 101
Pretax profit, 157
Price/Book ratio (P/B), 182–184
Price/Cash ratio (P/C), 184–185
Price/Sales ratio (P/S), 181–182
PricewaterhouseCoopers, 58
Procter & Gamble, 131
Prudential, 68, 166
Public Accounting Oversight Board, 65

Quaker Oats, 112
Quick assets ratio, 143

Random Walk Hypothesis, 45–47
Ratios, 8, 137–139, 155–157
Recognition principle, 98
Reserve for bad debts, 101–102, 146–147
Resistance level, 38, 197
Return on equity, 156
Reuters, 195
Revenues, 20, 108–109, 156–157
Risk, 47–55, 188–190
Roll-up strategy, 88
Runaway gap, 196–197

S&P 500 index, 44, 122, 194
Sarbanes-Oxley Act of 2002 (SOX),
     64–67
SBC Communications, 206
Sears, 170–171
Securities and Exchange Commission (SEC)
     Chairman Pitt, 62
     filings, 132, 144
     fines assessed, 68
     investigation of Xerox, 57
     Waste Management and, 88
     website, 61
     W. R. Grace and, 115
Segment, 157
Shareholder Relations Department, 89, 93
Simple moving average, 9–10
Snapple, 112
Sources of funds, 23–24
Specialist, 50
Spikes, 39, 189
Standard & Poor's Corporation,
     72, 116–117, 177
Starbucks Coffee, 166
STARS Report, 177, 195

Statement of cash flows, 23–26
Statement of operations, 18–22
Stock options, 114
Stub period, 88
Subsidiary, 158
Sugar bowl accounting, 95
Sunbeam, 109, 116, 199
Support level, 38, 197

Taco Bell, 166
Tangible book value per share, 182–183
Target, 131, 164, 170
Tax risk, 53, 207–209
Technical analysis, 34–39, 124–126, 187
10-Q filings, 132, 144
3M, 131
Tootsie Roll, 131
Total capitalization, 83
Toys "R" Us, 116
Trading range, 38
Trends, 9, 134–136, 157–164, 185–186
Triangles, 39
Tyco, 58, 106

United Mobile Homes, 206
Unrecorded liabilities, 91, 153–154
U.S. Robotics, 116
Utah International, 110

V formations, 39
Volatility, 188–190

W. R. Grace, 115
Wall Street Journal, 43
Wal-Mart, 164, 170
Walt Disney Company, 116
Washington Mutual, 206
Waste Management, Inc., 88
Weighted moving average, 10–13
Working capital, 25, 70, 140–147
WorldCom, 106
Wriston, Walter, 61
Write-off, 102

Xerox, 57, 83, 106, 199

Yield, 156